FOLLOWING WELL

Understand The Followership Principles

That Make Life Work

FOLLOWING WELL

Understand The Followership Principles That
Make Life Work

OMOKHAI IMOUKHUEDE PH.D.

LIMOUX
PUBLISHERS

Following Well:

Understand The Followership Principles That Make Life Work

ISBN 13: 978-0-578-73312-8

Copyright© 2020 by Omokhai Imoukhuede Ph.D.

Published by Limoux Publishers

Chicago, IL 60620

Interior Design: Limoux Publishers

Exterior Book Cover Design: Kachi Ukuru

Edited by Emi Aprekumah

To my wife Osen,

My children, Alina, Sophia, Hannah, and Jeremiah.

To every leadership and followership practitioner.

CONTENTS

INTRODUCTION

"No matter who is memorialized as founder, no nation or organization is built without the collective effort of a group of able, energetic, unsung followers" – Warren Bennis

"**I** am not a follower."
"Oh, I don't follow. I lead."
"Following is for sheep. I'm a leader."

These were the types of responses I heard whenever I discussed the merits of followership in the church. Unfortunately, I had heard rebukes of followership everywhere—not just in the church. Over and over again, I hear parents telling their children to never be followers and this cycle continues with children as I often hear them teasing each other for being "followers" in playgrounds and parties.

Children, it seems, have gotten the message their parents want them to be leaders.

Their schools want them to be leaders. So, does almost every tweet, meme, movie, comic book, and cartoon. Everything, it seems, is pushing the narrative that suggests leadership as the only status to which one should aspire. In addition to this narrow devotion to leadership, people are often disillusioned because of their past experiences when following.

I consistently hear complaints about people's disappointments in the leaders or causes they have followed in the past. As I encountered these negative feelings, it dawned on me that there is still work to do. There is an acute need for a "blue ocean strategy[1]"—a strategic effort to go against the cultural and intellectual grain of only learning about leadership.

Therefore, we must spend time speaking a truth that has long been left behind as our culture increasingly popularizes leadership studies as the starting point in both the Kingdom and in the world. Consequently, despite my initial reservations, I felt led to write a follow-up book on my initial book on followership—to lend my voice to a startlingly narrow genre of nonfiction literature.

As I researched, I discovered some positive occurrences since my first book 'Discovering Followership' was published. Over the last ten years from 2010 to 2020 as at writing this book, there has been a relatively increased focus on the subject of followership, especially within academia. Several research works published in dissertations and leadership journals on followership prove this increased focus.

On a personal note, my journey as a Ph.D. student studying leadership during this period also exposed me to classes that included the study of followership which were traditionally not included in the doctoral leadership studies curriculum. These classes subsequently influenced my doctoral dissertation which was a research that examined the impact of entrepreneurial leadership on authentic followership in the United States and Nigeria.

Lastly, in my numerous training and consultancy sessions on followership, I am consistently humbled by the positive feedback I receive. Numerous participants in these sessions have expressed the impact learning about followership has had on their lives and organizations.

While it is encouraging that an increased number of academics and laypeople are beginning to appreciate the importance of studying followership, the consensus among social scientists and leadership experts is that more study on the subject is still needed and must be encouraged[2].

A quick review of any leadership database website still shows a significant disparity in the number of materials focused on leadership compared to the number of materials on follow-ership.

For instance, a Google Scholar database word search of 'fol-lowership' yields 25,100 results. A similar search for 'leader-ship', on the other hand, yields more than 4 million results. Alt-hough one can argue that leadership materials or even books in-herently include a discussion on followership, this disparity highlights a gap as well as an opportunity that requires the in-clusion of more materials directly focused on the explorations of followership.

The goal of this book is not necessarily to seek equality in the focus between leadership and followership. Rather, contex-tual themes may dictate which of the two subjects to empha-size[3]. Moreover, in earlier books and materials on followership, the question about why there is a disparity in focus and whether or not this gap is worth bridging has been addressed[4]. Also, the impact of gender on the leadership-followership rela-tionship is beyond the scope of this book and not discussed since research reveals that gender as a variable on leadership-followership relationship shows very little significance[5].

With this in mind, my approach in this book is to evaluate this phenomenon by intimately studying the subject matter uti-lizing an authentic and balanced view of the subject matter of followership with the application of relevant Biblical truths. In essence, just as it is important to learn and understand how to lead well (avoid bad leadership), it is also important to learn and understand what it means to follow well.

This book takes off from where I left off in my previous book and seeks to answer some questions that I was not able to address in my first book on followership. I encourage you to read my initial work "Discovering Followership" as well as utilize the accompanying study guide for this book to complement your reading. These would serve as good materials and building blocks to enhancing your understanding of the subject matter. My prayer is that as you read, you will grasp the intricacies of followership, understand it contextually and apply the principles for maximum impact in your life, initiative, or organization. Happy reading.

Omokhai Imoukhuede, Ph.D.

CHAPTER ONE

Understanding the Power of Followership

"Man is always inclined to be intolerant towards the thing, or person,
he hasn't taken the time adequately to understand"
– Robert R. Brow

T he public's lack of interest in followership most likely stems from a lack of understanding[1]. This understanding of followership—a comprehension, enlightenment about, or deep familiarity with followership—would lead to empowerment. Our familiarity with a particular tool or a language creates confidence in using that tool or language. Familiarity leads to action. Therefore, as our familiarity with, or understanding of followership grows, so will our ability to apply followership principles in our daily lives.

We see this principle in the scriptures. Psalm 119:34 says, "*Give me understanding, and I will obey your instructions; I will put them into practice with all my heart*" (NLT).

1

In this verse, understanding is directly linked to the ability to act. That is, understanding, enlightenment or familiarity leads to the ability to apply a rule correctly. Therefore, correct applications of Biblical principles, like followership, require deep understanding.

A shallow awareness of a principle cannot lead to the correct application of it. Therefore, in our quest to become effective at utilizing Biblical followership principles, our initial goal must be to achieve a higher level of familiarity with the underlying principles and objectives of followership.

I use the word quest because this is a journey that will take effort and simple, passing knowledge is not the foundation of true followership. Albert Einstein once said, *"Any fool can know, the point is to understand."* Seeking that understanding is the bulk of the work in our quest.

So, how do we go about this? How do we become intimately familiar with followership? The first step in any quest is the desire to go on the journey. To embrace the journey entirely with a realization of the significance and power of the process.

Accept the Importance and Power of Followership

This process begins, when we accept the importance and power of followership in our lives.

As Barbara Kellerman stated in her book titled *Followership: How Followers Are Creating Change and Changing Leaders*, "followership is a human condition that we all engage in passively or actively"[2]. Therefore, whether or not you ever seek to understand and effectively follow Biblical principles concerning followership, you are already engaging in some sort of degree of followership. That is your activity or passivity in engaging in followership directly impacts the power your followership wields.

Hence, to approach and be able to utilize the fullness of the power of followership, we must then actively seek to engage in followership.

When something is important to us, we pay close attention to it, engaging in it more actively. Understanding the importance and power of followership will reflect the degree to which we engage in following well. It reveals our commitment and our willingness to pursue goals, visions, and various endeavors.

Ultimately, to begin the process of understanding, we must accept the important place followership occupies on the "leadership table".

Accept That Followers Have Tremendous Influence

Another important factor that helps our understanding is knowing that true followers are not just weaklings who "follow blindly" but, rather, are individuals with immense influence. In my earlier book, *Discovering Followership*, I mentioned that followers have influence and power they are often unaware of. If followership is properly engaged, it can propel a person, mission, or an organization's success.

We see this example in Jesus' disciples. Jesus proclaims that His followers would do greater things than He did while He walked on the earth[3]. We then see His disciples, in their humanity, embrace followership to different degrees. The effectiveness of the disciples' followership demonstrably had a direct impact on the effectiveness of their ministries and their abilities to fulfill their callings.

For example, one of the disciples, Peter achieved success in preaching the gospel—reaching the Roman world at the time.

This success is a direct result of him following God's revelation that the gentile world was part of God's original plan for redemption. Peter's followership, therefore propelled the gospel, allowing it to reach the gentile world, laying a foundation for other believers like Apostle Paul who ended up writing two-thirds of the New Testament. These later disciples had a foundation to build on and were able to make the gospel a global phenomenon, in part, because of their ability to embrace followership. Their realization that followership was the route to influence was crucial to their success.

Therefore, in an atmosphere of effective leadership and followership, influence is imparted on both sides. Great leaders' influence is transferred and shared with followers to the extent that these followers embrace the principles of followership. The implication is that our familiarity and understanding of leadership are incomplete without a corresponding knowledge and understanding of followership and the impact a leader has generally is in direct relationship with the impact that their followers can reflect on their world[4].

Relinquish Preconceived Notions about Followership

To engage the power in understanding followership, we must conduct an in-depth analysis of the subject with an open mind. This means that initially, though it may be uncomfortable to delve into the idea that you are meant to excel at the act of following, it's important to wade through this discomfort.

You must realize that over and over again our cultures have primed us to be disdainful of being followers.

Because of years of exposure to this negativity, there is most likely already a predisposition against following embedded in you. There is a natural barrier to understanding followership and, ultimately embracing followership. As I prod you to engage in an analysis of followership, these biases will most likely immediately rise to defend against you accepting followership.

Therefore, to be successful on your quest, you must put aside pre-judgments and any biases about followership or what it means to be a follower. We must be open to the idea that a) we were made to follow and b) following has a much wider construct than we have been led to believe.

Embrace Humility

In addition to openness, we need humility to understand followership. Every act of true Biblical followership is rooted in humility, it is difficult to learn about followership if you are not embarking on the quest in humility.

Writing to the Philippians, Apostle Paul says, "*Do nothing out of selfish ambition or vain conceit. Rather, in humility value others above yourselves, not looking to your interests but each of you to the interests of the others*" (Philippians 2:3-4).

This means, as followers, you will have to put aside your immediate interests and, instead, focus on the bigger picture, the needs of the most vulnerable, and/or the ultimate goal.

These acts would seem absurd, shortsighted, or foolish to someone who is not operating in humility. A lack of humility can immediately impede any effort to become familiar with followership. A sole focus on self is antithetical to followership. Therefore, it cannot abide and must be replaced by humility on any serious quest towards effective followership.

My Quest

When I first started trying to understand followership, I dug into my life to try to figure out where my preconceived notions of followership came from. I realized that my initial perceptions of followership were shaped by my early experiences with leadership and followership. I was raised in Nigeria and witnessed several military dictatorships.

The masses, as we referred to the populace, did not have many rights. Any protest was met with brutal punishment, which in some cases, led to death. So, people rarely tried to assert the few rights they had. In this setting, leaders lived in extravagant homes, their children attended the best schools and traveled the globe living lavishly, while most of the Nigerian masses lived modestly or in abject poverty.

When I was growing up it seemed, to me, that the followers had the short end of the stick. They were simply zombies and hired hands who operated like machines and danced to the drums of the employers or leaders.

So, like most people where I grew up, my aspirations were simple, I sought leadership so that I could enjoy the perks, not out of any desire to serve. It was accepted at that stage in life that leaders enjoyed life at the expense of followers.

This leader-centric culture surrounded me, even in my personal life. I was the oldest of six children. I was assumed to be the de-facto leader and all the other children were supposed to defer to me. Amongst the six of us, there was a chain of command with me at the head. I was preoccupied with ensuring everyone respected me and followed my lead.

This approach to leadership affected my self-esteem and built numerous insecurities in me. Any form of pushback or feedback—from, first my siblings, and then others as I went into the greater world—seemed to be an attack on me.

Because I could only see myself as a leader with power, any difference of opinion—was an attack on that power, the biggest part of my identity at the time.

As a result, I did not have much patience or empathy for my younger siblings, especially when I felt they were being disrespectful to me.

As I grew older, I began to experience the other side of the equation when I arrived at Federal Government College Warri, my dream high school. At the time, many of the guys in the neighborhood that I admired attended the school. I remember thinking they were so cool. I admired their crisp white long sleeve shirts paired sharply with white dress slacks and black shoes. I was also drawn to the academic excellence of the students.

So, I was extremely excited when I found out I was admitted to the school. However, all my excitement would end on my first day in this boarding school.

In this setting, as a freshman, I was no longer the top dog, but was under the authority and brute mercy of the seniors in my boarding school. The school's hierarchical culture was upheld by consistent bullying. First-year students were the lowest of the low end of the hierarchical pole and reminded of it regularly. Seniors ruthlessly exerted their power, terrorizing us first-year students at will.

For example, when I arrived on the first day, we were all rounded up in a room and told to bring out all our provisions –

school supplies and food. Resistance to this request by our seniors was met with serious punishment and beatings.

By the end of the first week, my belongings were no longer mine and my provisions were confiscated by older students. While carrying out our daily school lives, first years could be randomly stopped by seniors who would demand that we wash or iron their clothes, fetch water for them or carry out any other type of manual labor.

Friday nights were the worst. Friday night was "ground-work night", the night when we were supposed to clean up the hostel. This cleaning exercise usually began around 10 pm and would end early in the mornings.

Sometimes as a form of punishment, seniors would tell us to lie on the cold concrete floors for hours or would beat us when our hostels did not do well in the inspections. One would think that these experiences were those of young military recruits. But, we were not in a military school.

We were just pre-teens who were being systematically traumatized by older students. When we tried to complain to our teachers, it seemed like our complaints were ignored. Students who had connections were able to transfer out of the school. But, that was not the case for most students, including me.

So, we accepted this life and just suffered through the process.

The primary goal of every first-year student in my high school, especially the guys, was to survive. Sadly, first-year students' endurance was bolstered by the hope of one day exerting the same punishment on the rookies when we became seniors.

This experience opened my eyes to the feelings, perceptions, and survival techniques of a follower within an unfair hierarchical and despotic leadership system.

In addition to the stress of being consistently bullied, I often felt a bitter taste in my mouth as I witnessed first-year students scheming for the approval of the seniors.

For example, some students would lie about other students just to make themselves look good in front of an influential senior. Others offered provisions and even bribed their way into the good graces of these seniors or for their protection. First years faked commitment and loyalty to these seniors just to save themselves from punishment.

Many were no longer authentic about their true feelings about the conditions and simply just went with the flow. What saved me was my faith, genuine friendships developed with my classmates, and the timely interventions of some well-intended seniors (luckily, not all seniors were bad). I survived freshman year and eventually graduated high school in one piece but was marked by my experiences.

As I moved on into adulthood, through college and my initial work experiences. I saw the same problematic relationships between leaders and followers.

When I immigrated to the United States, it became clear these fraught leader-follower relationships were a global phenomenon. At work, I saw two camps, corporate (seniors) and employees (freshmen, juniors). Corporate (seniors) harshly trying to ensure employees (freshmen) aligned with organizational goals and followers (freshmen, juniors) not being happy about working conditions and business processes.

Despite their unhappiness, I saw employees scheming and politicking for the very positions they resented within corporate America. Keeping quiet, when they were supposed to speak up against injustice, being disengaged, and just picking up a paycheck. In these spaces, as part of the "rat race," I continued to see followership as a forced condition of servitude.

What changed? As my calling kept leading me into hybrid leader-follower spaces, I began to ask questions about what followership meant to me. In those spaces I was forced to confront all the baggage I had about following (and, to some extent leading). I dug into my feelings about roles and pondered the importance of followers in general.

I allowed myself room to accept an honest answer, answers no one had given me before.

I opened myself to both the good and the bad connotations of followership and let it rip. Among other things, I thought of every time I was forced to wash seniors' plates or iron their school clothes. I also ran through every time I had demanded complete obedience and thought of how each person under "my command" had responded.

As I became open, I experienced freedom, a powerful release from the boundaries set by my painful experiences with followership. I began to realize what followership could be in an ideal setting and became secure in my followership. It became clear that followership is much more than a label, role, rank, or title; it is a liberating process when it is a response to a calling—a mission, an idea, a task, vision, or a word from God our creator.

A world of possibility arose for me once I accepted this call to follow. I felt guided and had a new sense of purpose and direction. In this time of transparency, where I was no longer trapped by past experiences with bad leadership and the resulting examples of unhealthy followership, I gained a posture of humility and a spirit of authenticity.

CHAPTER TWO

The God Factor

"It is the Lord your God you must follow, and him you must revere.
Keep his commands and obey him; serve him and hold fast to him"
– Deuteronomy 13:4.

Our purpose and significance begin with God. There is wisdom in seeking ideas beyond what you can conceive. While there are heights we can achieve on our own, to fully gain understanding in this world, we must reach out to the source of this world.

There undoubtedly are secular paths to followership. But, much like every other topic, the "God factor" takes followership to a different level.

Inner Calls

Followership cannot be fully understood, without acknowledging that God is our source and that God is the one who has set us on our paths. There is an origin to all the dreams, all the aspirations, and all the goals we have. There is an inner call to greatness, to follow dreams that are beyond us that influence us to take steps.

Ultimately, life itself is a call to followership. It is a call to follow these God giving inner-promptings. Each person has internal calls that are not necessarily explainable. We see people training for years to climb mountains and achieve incredible feats in research and athletics. When you ask them about their inspiration, they often talk about an unquantifiable inner drive which first led them to desire the result and propelled them through the immense work it took them to arrive at the goal.

Our quest, towards effective followership, relies on us being aware that there are promptings only our spiritual sensitivities can perceive. These inner callings, or promptings, arouse a desire for something more profound than our typical physical or mental understandings. These promptings lead us to acknowledge God, thus beginning our quest in followership.

Our first true act of followership, therefore, begins with the simple desire to acknowledge God, to acknowledge those internal promptings suggesting greater levels of existence (our purpose).

These motivations for transcendent pursuit, or promptings, continue incessantly, regardless of our knowledge of God.

The knowledge of God, however, can tether those prompt-ings, to true goodness and things of lasting value. The knowledge of God gives quality to the decision and effort to fol-low. There is some inner validation of our followership process when we acknowledge God.

Yes, experiences, family backgrounds, and world views play a huge role in our followership quest, however, without an un-derstanding of God's place as the source and center of life itself, important promptings like followership may fall to the way-side, or be adhered to ineffectively. The famous Christian apol-ogist Ravi Zacharias of blessed memory often explained this concept differently by saying, "We cannot accept moral law without the acceptance of the moral lawgiver!".

In other words, our desire to follow or do what we perceive as morally right based on our inner values or promptings is in-fluenced by the source of those promptings and that's God. In essence, our acts towards morally right activity are in itself a reflection of our followership to God. This thirst for the law and the lawgiver behind the law can be seen in our daily lives.

We are continually asking questions and are constantly studying what already exists to understand what is not under-stood or perceived physically.

The great philosopher, Plato, said, "It is clear to everyone that astronomy at all events compels the soul to look upwards, and draws it from the things of this world to the other[2]."

In Romans 1:20, Apostle Paul renders this sentiment accordingly, *"for since the creation of the world God's invisible qualities—his eternal power and divine nature—have been seen, being understood from what has been made, so that people are without excuse."*

When we examine the lives of people that have a strong sense of followership, we find that they are following the person of God wholeheartedly, or they are merely applying and following Godly principles.

Several studies demonstrate this concept. For example, research on spiritual leadership by Louis W. Fry shows how strongly our spirituality reflects our acceptance of transcendent notions and influences our actions and reactions to others, especially in the workplace[3].

The more we respond to higher spiritual authority or promptings positively, the more we reflect God's ways of doing things.

We truly understand who we are by accepting that our service to humanity reflects standards of morality that are traced to God. In essence, our 'employment' or call has its source in God as Christian leaders.

Work and service must be seen as a fundamental response to God's call for us to love and support one another. When we respond to this call, we become stewards of the supernatural promptings we get. The implication of this is that eventually, we shall give an account of our actions because our followership response is a response not only to humanity but also, and most especially, a response to God.

In Ephesians 6:5-8, Paul admonishes the Ephesian church, urging them to see their service to others as a service to God and not man. In this section, Paul concluded that masters, employees, and/or leaders were to treat those who worked for or followed them as fellow servants who report to the same God.

The bottom line is that following is a privilege and an act of stewardship towards the unseen (God, the goal, vision, ideal) to whom we will give an account at the end of the day. Our posture before God as followers—people who admit they don't have all the answers—acknowledges our subordination to God, our creator, as the source of all things, including our call to followership.

CHAPTER THREE

Understanding Context

"I do not fear the truth. I welcome it. But I wish all of my facts to be in their proper context." – Gordon B. Hinckley

To understand how to follow well, we have to examine the context in which we find ourselves. Following well should be approached as a process, behavior, and also perception based on the lens and context that the leader, follower, idea, vision, or goal is located in[1].

The context within the realm of followership means, the conditions, culture, and the overall environment that the following occurs. Following is multi-dimensional and occurs within different conditions, cultures, and environments.

These conditions include the type of organization (corporate vs nonprofit), the spiritual sensitivities within leadership, level of toxicity and harmony, economic and social conditions, country, organizational culture, the type of leadership style, type of followership style and the environment (volatile, crisis-prone, stress levels).

The reality is that different contexts call for various applications and perceptions of followership[2]. The mistake we make is that we are either unaware of the conditions, cultures, and overall environment in which our followership occurs or we apply rules specific to a particular context to an entirely different set of variables within another context. While this may sound like a no brainer, I am often amazed at how leaders and followers alike violate this truth, which points to an overall lack of understanding in this area.

My Quest

Sarah, a very skilled, qualified, and accomplished professional is offered her dream job as an executive. She is excited about the opportunity but realized immediately on her first day that there are some process gaps within the organization. Communication from leadership to middle management was not organized, there was serious mismanagement of time. After about a week in the organization, her quiet observations turned into frustrating sighs and looks of bewilderment.

As time went on, she tried on her own to completely overhaul the processes and culture, what she did not expect was aggressive push back from other executive members (typical response right?).

Though she tried often to make changes in the organizations, Sarah failed to communicate her changes effectively because she did not consider the context she was in. She came from a company in which she had autonomy and was able to make decisions and changes with very little push back from her superiors. She always felt empowered to make decisions without micromanagement, however in this company, there was a tight grip on top.

Despite this change, she continued to use the communication methods she was used to in her other company and experienced considerable frustration as she struggled to make her mark in her new role. She did not look into the culture, history and environmental factors, the capacity and ability of the staff she worked with, and the leadership style of her immediate boss. Within a few months, she quit her job. The context was everything.

The followership techniques that had propelled her career in the past could no longer suffice because the context had changed.

A failure to appreciate context plays a role in non-corporate spheres as well. There are many stories of the negative effects of the savior complex when Christian missionaries or philanthropist arrive at their destination. Despite their intent to help a group, these missionaries and philanthropists face rejection or failure because they did not learn the context they were in before offering suggestions for help. Their lack of adherence or followership to the cultures and norms of the societies that they were in and prevalent religious practices prevented positive responses from the locals and at times spurred resistance to their influence.

Apostle Paul in his epistle to the Corinthian church expressed his understanding of the power of context when he posited that he became all things to all men to impact them for Christ regardless of their contexts, as Jews, gentiles, strong or weak[3]. Contextual consideration leans itself toward empathy, emotional intelligence, and the acceptance that our responses to leadership—or anyone, for that matter—must be approached with understanding.

As Paul sought to follow God's will that he share the gospel, he learned and responded to each context in which he found himself. This phrase, "I became", suggests a willingness to follow and understand what the existing context is calling for.

Here are some contextual frameworks to consider that help us follow well. I have kept these contextual frameworks to two because I believe these two encapsulate the others.

For example, the spiritual and religious context includes social contexts while cultural contexts influence and include environmental, subcultural, and even the technological context.

Spiritual Context

The spiritual context of an organization is linked to spiritual sensitivities and spiritual motivations of the leaders and followers within an organization[4]. Each person has a spirituality, or spiritual sensibilities, tied to their values. Spiritual sensibilities are based on our experiences and interpretations of our world that enable us to determine what is right or wrong and reflect attitudes of love, respect, empowerment, generosity[5,] etc.

As spiritual beings, the spiritual sensibilities of leaders and followers, often guide their style and help define the spiritual context that surrounds the relationship or vision.

For instance, Steve Jobs' spiritual sensibilities were widely publicized and seemed to prioritize minimalism, self-empowerment, and wellness[6]. Therefore, it's not a coincidence that we saw the company culture as well as product design skew in these directions.

The same goes for Oprah Winfrey and Bill Gates, these leaders' spiritual bend seemed to directly affect how they run their businesses.

Chick-fil-A leader and founder the late Truett Cathy had spiritual sensibilities that were tied to Christian values that spilled over to organizational culture. Karl Wierk's work on cognitive processes in organizations supports the assertion that although employees or followers come into an organization with specific individual goals or spiritual sensibilities, after a while, many followers' goals expand to incorporate their leaders' goals[7].

Though there are many exceptions to this principle—as many followers do not go on to incorporate their leaders' goals or spiritual sensibilities—it is important to understand how the spiritual context affects followership.

For example, a disconnection between an individual's sense of spirituality espoused values, and actual practiced values can lead to disagreement within the leader-follower relationship.

Even Christian non-profit organizations are not exempt from the disharmony that comes when leaders and followers are not aligned in their expression and practice of spiritual sensibilities.

If these spiritual differences are not properly addressed, there may be disharmony within the organization which may cause followers to doubt the authenticity of their leaders and overall vision.

Followers, therefore, in this context, must gain an in-depth understanding of the spiritual context by taking the initiative to investigate the overall spiritual essence of their organization.

How do we determine this? Given that our spiritual sensibilities are expressed in human acts of gratitude, generosity, kindness, compassion, empowerment and humility[8], a simple way is to examine, how espoused values, acts of kindness, generosity, empathy, integrity, honesty and love are practiced by both leaders and followers.

Followers must also take a close look at how leaders and followers interact with individuals outside their environment to review inconsistencies or consistencies between espoused values and actual behavior.

Religious Context

The second context to consider is the religious context, which is the religious environment the leadership and followership occur in.

This also has to do with norms and beliefs systems tied to religion that influence how leaders and followers interact.

For example, during the United States presidential election in 1959 between the then incumbent Vice President Richard Nixon and then Senator John F. Kennedy, it was believed that one of the underlying factors that propelled Kennedy to victory was the influx of the Roman Catholic vote[9].

At that time, there had not been a Roman Catholic President and there were some concerns that John F. Kennedy's Roman Catholic background would affect his leadership within the mostly protestant American citizenry. Although Kennedy worked hard to alleviate these concerns and narrowly won the election against Nixon, the point was clear that anyone seeking to lead America had to understand the dynamics of religious context within the political landscape of the country. Interestingly, this perception is just as important in politics today as it was in 1959 as politicians seek to appeal to religious sensitivities to obtain votes.

Another example was with missionaries hoping to spread Christianity to indigenes of northern Nigeria in the early 19th century. Missionaries during this period, faced tremendous resistance due to the existence of Islam within the cultural fabric of the villages. Islam had been the primary religion in the area and had existed five centuries before Christianity[10].

With Islam deeply entrenched in the psyche of the indigenes there was added resistance to what these missionary hoped to achieve.

While there were pockets of successes, the message was clear, religious context played an important role in understanding why people resisted the call to convert to Christianity.

The impact of religious context plays out in international politics as well. For example, though the United Kingdom and the United States, at various times, have professed to be 'Christian' nations, the manner in which these countries' leadership have expressed this spirituality in light of their religious norms and beliefs is very different. Even the way these countries practice religion locally is also extremely different.

For example, both nations have dominant political parties designated as right or left leaning parties. Despite this identical designation, left leaning or right leaning, these parties are vastly different, in part because of the different expression of religious beliefs and norms within these countries.

Therefore, a left leaning politician who is very successful in one of the nations could fail woefully in the other local region or country if the politician is not aware of the subtle differences in spiritual and this case religious context. One nation may embrace a left leaning politician who openly talks about God and the need to adhere to Biblical principles, while the other nation may be uncomfortable with such directness and lean more favorably to politicians who embrace these Biblical principles without expressly tying these principles to the Christian faith. Thus, religious sensitivity, an awareness of the religious context, can be the difference between success and failure—thriving and mere existence in the political arena. Outside politics, having this awareness creates the flexibility for followers to make adjustments in their behaviors, responses and actions especially in spaces with different religious environments.

Going back to Apostle Paul's letter to the Corinthian church in 1 Corinthians 9:19-23, we see Paul making adjustments in his interactions with non-believing Greeks. Paul's religious sensitivity to the spiritual state of those he engaged with, determined the type of follower he was within those settings. It determined his overall engagement in light of his new revelation from Christ as a lover of humanity. Jews and gentiles were not the same in their spiritual orientation, sensitivities, religions and motivations, however, Paul's understanding of these differences enabled him to be effective as a servant of the gospel to these individuals. Apostle Paul became what the religious context called for without losing his authenticity and originality while being empathetic.

Cultural and subcultural Context

Cultural context is the perception of the way a group feels, thinks and acts based on patterns of thinking that distinguishes one group from another[11]. An awareness of cultural context is an understanding of the personality of the group and its accepted traditions.

Within organizations, these are rules of engagement based on historically accepted approaches which are influenced by several factors, including environmental, societal, ecological, and political tendencies.

Therefore, cultural context includes the conditions that exist for patterns of thinking, feelings and traditions within the leadership followership relationship. Several studies have sought to understand how followers respond to leadership within various cultures.

A very important study on how culture influences leadership-followership perceptions is the GLOBE study[12]. According to the GLOBE study, cultures with high affinity for power, that concentrate power at the top, tend to approach followership differently than cultures with low affinity for power[14]. In high power distance cultures, such as in counties in Sub-Saharan Africa like Nigeria, leaders are perceived to wield power while followers tend to be more subservient and less participatory.

This may explain my initial take on followership. There is a pattern of thinking in the area of power within many Nigerian cultures that affects the way followers respond to varying leadership styles.

According to the GLOBE study, in these cultures, there are sharp delineations between those in power and those who do not have control. There are also leadership preferences; those preferences often guide follower's views on leadership effectiveness. Therefore, although citizens in high power distance cultures may desire more participatory leadership, autocratic leadership tends to prevail in these cultures.

The cultural context supersedes personal desires, resulting in a default preference of autocratic leadership[13]. On the other hand, in low power distance countries, such as the United States, power is not so distant from those who follow and, as such, generally and with few exceptions; followership is somewhat participatory. Participatory models, therefore, tend to be the default—even in situations where individuals may prefer autocratic leadership.

Therefore, having a basic understanding of these cultural dimensions within organizations and nations goes a long way to improve our overall followership.

Much like a nation has an overall culture that encourages dedicated and effective followership, many organizations and affiliations within a nation also have cultural contexts that directly affect followership.

For example, the way members of the American army follow may be different from the way gang members or church members follow leadership because these sub cultural groups are different. In different countries, members of these same groups may have other cultural contexts to consider as they follow[14]. Therefore, to be successful, these followers must identify their current cultural context, learn the rules of engagement and then follow accordingly.

Cultural Competency in Practice

Cultural context was especially important when I lived in Europe in the late-90s. I had an internship opportunity working for one of the largest oil companies in Madrid Spain at the time. I remember being picked up by my bosses as we drove 35mins to the beautiful office complex.

After I had settled in, I immediately noticed the relaxed atmosphere. The office had an open floor plan where everyone could see one another. This was very different from my past work experience in Nigeria where bosses had separate offices and a closed door policy. At the oil company, though there was a chain of command and respect, everyone related freely—both bosses and subordinates mingled freely engaged in office comradery.

Outside the office, I observed how people greeted and related to one another. Friends who were of the opposite sex would greet each other with two kisses and if you were introduced to a member of the opposite sex and mistakenly gave one kiss on the cheek, depending on the familiarity, the recipient would politely chide, "Dos besos por favor"—two kisses, please. Coming from Nigeria, this type of greeting was starkly different from what I was used to. In Nigerian work settings when you first met someone, you simply shook hands. Over time, familiarity would allow for a "church hug"—a brief side hug of sorts that limited contact. You certainly never would give a person you just met two kisses, especially if the person was of the opposite sex at least not in my day.

Another aspect of work culture that was different in Spain was the daily work hours. Each day there was a two-hour lunch period which included time for a nap. In Spain, at that time, everything shut down from 2pm to 4pm for lunch. In most Nigerian companies at the time, lunch breaks were more of an after-thought. In Madrid, workers returned to work at 4pm and worked till 8:30pm. Most people then had dinner at 10pm.

Work ethic is measured differently in a culture that afforded two-hour lunches and late dinners. When I later moved to the

United States, I discovered that there were rarely any two-hour lunches except on scheduled lunch meetings with team members. The lunch culture signaled other differences in work expectations, including staff relationships. In each culture, I had to adjust my followership style in order for me to be successful, and to enjoy the benefits of each organization.

Our Posture before Our Current Context

I am always amazed at followers who fail to take the time to understand the context that they find themselves in. It seems as if their desires to engage their environment immediately overshadows the need to learn from the context in which they are located. From my experience, such followers either end up leaving the environment or face increased push back from the environment. Taking time to learn your environment, taking time to ask questions, taking time to know what is appropriate and what is not appropriate, learning how to communicate what is needed within that context are ways to identify with the context within which followership occurs.

This will require humility, patience and a deep desire to learn about your environment. Jesus, again, is an example of this process of humility and learning. Luke 2:46-47 says that "*...after three days they found him in the temple courts, sitting among the teachers,* *listening to them and asking them questions. Everyone who heard him was amazed at his understanding and his answers,"* Christ's posture as a young boy at age 12 was not one of arrogance but listening and learning by asking questions. Although He was the Savior of the world, Jesus learnt context by asking questions and learning, a process that preceded the revelation of Christ's wisdom and made His answers relatable. John 1:14 also says that *"The Word became flesh and dwelt among men."* This means, Jesus embraced our context as human beings, dwelling within this cultural and spiritual context in which He found himself. This enabled him to effectively follow God's instructions and redeem humankind.

As a result, none of Jesus' words were wasted. When he spoke to fishermen, He utilized their context to teach. When He engaged the woman at the well, He related to her in her unique context, addressing her relationships and status as a foreigner. Over and over again, we see Jesus understanding the fullness of context and then teaching accordingly.

The lessons He provides Pharisees are different from the messages he provides to fisherman and are necessarily different from the messages He provides to tax collectors. He fundamentally understood that each person's ability to grasp and follow started with his understanding of context.

CHAPTER FOUR

Understanding Whom to Follow

"Followers have noted, tested, and refined truisms by carefully study-ing the leaders they chose to follow" – Dumoulin

M ost followership experts agree that followership is a function of our wills, which means that we all have a choice of whom or what we follow. How-ever, deciding who or what to follow may be a complicated and sometimes tedious process. Especially, today—with the pres-ence of media that allows us to engage a wider breadth of knowledge—we are inundated with so many choices, options and paths. For instance, social media is filled with a multitude of influencers using these platforms to espouse a wide array of philosophies.

This overload of options, voices and actors in the inspira-tional and motivational scene leaves the untrained and unin-formed subject to misinformation.

It leaves many people vulnerable to individuals who may take advantage of their naivety. Same is applicable to politics or any other field for that matter. Making a decision on what church to be a member of, what career path to take, what group to join or what causes to engage in are questions many of us have wrestled with in our lives. Getting answers to these questions are also not easy. As a result, numerous examples of followership gone awry exist.

For example, in the 1970s a group of followers of the cult leader Jim Jones committed mass suicide, in what is now known as the Jonestown massacre. Followers of many other socio-political groups, including Adolph Hitler's Nazi party and ISIS have similarly committed numerous acts harmful to themselves and others, all in the furtherance of bad followership[1].

This proliferation of bad followership (and by extension bad leaders) cannot be used as evidenced that followership itself is bad. Rather, it leads to the conclusion that certain types of followership are bad, and, therefore, followership cannot be entered into lightly. So how do we determine the best individuals or causes to follow?

What should our thought process be to determine this choice? What guidelines, if any, can we adopt when evaluating who or what to follow?

A good place to start is with a review of the impact of the leaders' vision, goals and mission on humanity. For my followership standards, I have decided that any person or idea that promotes the advancement of their worldview that improves conditions of service; or seeks the betterment of others—without physical, mental, spiritual or psychological harm to others—should be considered for followership.

This guide I use, necessarily depends on my values which are linked to my acceptance of Biblical standards of morality. Similarly, everyone following must have guides based on values that have an implicit definition of harm—or good vs. bad—included in their standard. Many times when we see bad followership it is not because the person does not know the difference between good or bad. It is usually because the person has not carefully reviewed their followership in terms of what they view as good or bad.

Simply put, if a leader's actions and promptings do not align with your personal identified standard for good or the leader's identified standard of good, it is important to reconsider that followership path. Therefore, we are to ask ourselves whether the ideas, missions, visions or individuals we intend to follow reflect a greater love for humanity and intention to improve humanity without first harming humanity.

If the leader reflects this love of humanity, exhibits motives intended to improve wellbeing and does not promote harmful behavior to others, then we can then proceed to the building blocks of our evaluation of whom to follow, an evaluation of what I call the Four Rs and Three Cs of whom to follow—Relevance, Relatability, Respect, Results and Character, Commitment, Conviction.

CHAPTER FIVE

The Relevance Factor

"Bring relevance to the people before teaching them to be believers"
— Sunday Adelaja

Evaluating relevance entails asking questions about the importance of that influencer, leader or mission to meeting your overall goals, aligning with your interests and contributing to the best use of your time.

Effective followers understand the impact of relevance and are constantly assessing the impact of promptings to follow on their overall goals, desires, pursuits, interests and objectives.

This means, that when deciding whether you should follow an individual, ideal or mission, you must make sure that who you're following is relevant—or has direct bearing—on the ultimate goal of your promptings, purpose and God's overall plan for you.

For example, I remember when considering job opportunities', I reviewed the mission, vision and overall impact of each organization to see how it aligned with my overall professional and altruistic goals.

As followers we must do some investigative work before we yield ourselves to the influence of others. We must also resist the temptation of just jumping into something just because of how it makes us feel, relevance must be considered.

There is a story in the Bible about Andrew's introduction to Jesus. Andrew was initially a disciple of John the Baptist who announced to his disciples that Jesus was the Messiah. Intrigued by this, Andrew sought to meet this Messiah. When Andrew finally meets Jesus, he asks to see where Jesus lived[1]. What sparked this interest? The relevance factor.

Jesus obliges and invites Andrew to his home. After spending time with Jesus, Andrew goes to his brother Peter to tell him about Jesus. On the surface this might seem like just the natural progression, however, when you examine the story critically, you will find that Andrew is taking time to confirm whether John's statements about Jesus were true.

He's also assessing Jesus to see whether it was worth his while to follow him. We see this assessment process with many other disciples, including Peter and Nathaniel.

They meet Jesus, review what he has said and, only then, do they begin to follow him. We then see that as they follow, these disciples continue to question Jesus, continually confirming that it still makes sense to follow Jesus. These disciples, especially Peter and Nathaniel's interest in following was solidified by Jesus' relevance to their immediate context, desires, needs, interests, stories and overall purpose in life. I remember going through a similar process when I first met my pastor and mentor.

I was at a point in my life where I was lacking direction about my purpose and needed some guidance on some steps to take so that my life's work would reflect the best use of my gifts. Therefore, I knew the mentor I needed at this point, must already be modeling what it is to effectively use gifts and must have a sense of how to lead someone to that understanding. Though this might sound like a selfish way to analyze followership, I contend that followership must engage our self-awareness but not selfishness.

That is, followership must align with your personal promptings or God given vision for yourself before it can blossom into an entity that serves others. Followership must tend to your strengths, strengthen your weaknesses and advance the essence of your existence.

If your followership is not meeting your personal needs or does not line up with the clear view of yourself or purpose, it is unlikely that you will ever effectively wield it to meet the needs of others.

In my case, I found my mentor's story as well as approach to life not only applicable to mine but also very pertinent to where I was going in life. I saw the relevance of what he brought to the table. In that vulnerable state, I knew I needed someone who would not be judgmental, but, instead, would gently guide me to the correct path. Once I saw this in my potential mentor, someone's whose life story, skillset and vision matched my needs, I saw a relevant leader and, therefore could assume followership.

The reality is that if your leader is not relevant to you, your followership will be undermined. When Jesus is asked about the validity of His ministry, He often responds by pointing at His relevance. For example, in response to John the Baptist's question, "Are you the one who is to come?[2]"—a question which essentially means, "Should we follow you?"—Jesus replies, "The blind receive sight, the lame walk, those who have leprosy are cleansed, the deaf hear, the dead are raised, and the good news is proclaimed to the poor"[3].

Therefore, Jesus answers John's question, "Are you the one I'm meant to follow" with a list of the issues people have and the relevance He, Jesus, has in these issues.

Thus, Jesus responds, "Yes, I'm the right one to follow if my ability to address these issues has any relevance in your life."

Alignment with Your Mission

A follower's perception of a leader's relevance and how that perception aligns with a follower's mission in life go hand in hand. To determine who to follow, followers must evaluate alignment with the causes, individuals, and ideas.

Like I mentioned earlier, when we examine the disciples we see them going through this process of evaluation of the alignment of goals and purpose. Some of them at first may have begun misaligned but when they encounter causes, leadership, missions that expose this misalignment, most times if honest, these followers end up seeking alignment that leads to the common good of others.

Peter is an example of this, when he met Jesus, his misalignment to his ultimate purpose was exposed. He humbly submitted to following Christ because he sought to realign himself with what Christ offered thus accepting Christ's relevance in his life. In essence, what makes a cause, a leader or mission relevant is alignment.

The ability of that leader, cause, or mission to align you with your original purpose, personal goals, interests, needs, and desires is what makes them relevant. Many are embarking on a misaligned mission which usually results in pain and disappointment and relevant leaders have a way to align people that follow them to something of interest be it recreational, secular, or eternal.

This type of alignment validates your choice, it encourages you to take the step of yielding your will towards the influence of the leader, cause, or ideal. On the other hand, if there is no value alignment, goal alignment, mission alignment, if there is no pertinence in what a leader brings to the table, then the followership will not be beneficial to you. The reality is that if leaders are not relevant to their followers, they lose their influence with those who follow them.

Connects With Your Interest

Following what interests us determines their level of relevance. We do not naturally follow what we are disinterested in. Relevance speaks to the level of interest a vision, leader, or mission generates in our lives.

Usually, when our interests are piqued, it is because of some results that we benefit from these things. For example, people follow whatever solves problems, addresses a sleepless night issue or something that brings joy and pleasure. The opposite feelings prevent any followership. The story of Andrew reflects these emotions of interest generated from the perception that Jesus was the Savior of the world. Another aspect of relevance has to do with whether or not you want to invest time in that person, cause, or thing.

Whatever, I give my time to, reflects its relevance to me and therefore determines what I follow. Usually, we just follow without examining the factors for relevance, however, the reality is that we are generally inspired to follow things that engage our time.

Motion

Followers must evaluate the relevance of their leaders, ideas, or visions by reviewing motion. A relevant leader moves their followers ahead in life and effective followership moves forward. There is a sense of progression in terms of personal, spiritual and mental development and advancement of the followers.

I once heard a statement someone said about followership, "if you are following someone who is in front of you and that person is not moving you ahead, then that person is an obstruction to your progress". In other words, a test of relevance is motion. Certain actions exhibited by leaders will demonstrate whether or not they are making progress and maturing in their area of specialty as well as advancing the lives of those who follow.

For example, if you followed someone because you felt an alignment with their mission of addressing pollution in the environment, you could measure movement by how much you have learned about environmental advocacy from the leader, or how much work you have been able to do, or how many initial goals you set with the leader, you have actually reached or are progressing towards meeting.

It may be helpful, when you first start following, to identify goals you hope to reach by following. You should set deadlines for these goals. From time to time you should review these goals and timelines. If you are not meeting them, it may be time to reassess your followership or put some intentionality in pursuing that movement.

Consistent Relevance

Relevance is time and season-specific. Relevant mentors when you are five and working on fitting into a kindergarten class, for instance, may no longer be relevant leaders as you decide a career path during your last year of college. In addition to your changes as a follower, that which you are following is also constantly changing and evolving. However in spite of these changes, we must also be on the lookout for consistency in messaging, in integrity, authenticity, and alignment with those we intend to follow.

For instance, a leader who was initially relevant in your quest to grow as a real estate investor for residential property may no longer be relevant if you have outgrown that space and are now focusing on commercial real estate. In this example, the mentor's expertise may be limited to residential property and if not updated may not be able to assist your quest to grow as an investor in commercial real estate. The consistency of learning from the mentor may be hindered because of this limitation of the leader.

I do believe that consistent relevance yields consistent followership. When I examine the likes of Dave Ramsey, John Maxwell, Oprah Winfrey, Elon Musk or rappers like Jay Z and Common, they have been able to maintain consistent followership because they have strived to be consistently relevant.

Meeting Your Needs

Another way to determine whether a leader is relevant is to assess whether or not the leader is actually meeting your felt needs. For instance, is the leader empathetic? Does the leader show you love? For example, if you have a family with young children, does the leader consider your family structure when working with you?

Do you feel supported by the leader when you explain your specific issues? Or, within the context of your followership, is the leader only able to give you general platitudes and never speak to your specific issues? Relevance, ultimately, is the merging of your goals, interest, and needs. For you to move forward in your destiny, your followership must always have a healthy balance of these.

The God Factor Revisited

The God Factor also has an impact on relevance. Our pursuit of God should dictate what we find relevant, and, therefore, what we follow. Jesus mentioned that when we seek God first, the ultimate source of our relevance, every other thing will be added to us[4]. This prioritization also determines what becomes relevant and what is not.

The God factor, then, demands that we have a clear definition and full understanding of our purpose, interests, needs, and values. This clarity, then guides what we deem relevant. Thus, the God factor may dramatically change the list of things, causes and people we follow. This plays out allowing God to lead us as we engage in prayers.

CHAPTER SIX

The Relatability Factor

"Your customers will always be human, always have an empathic ap-
proach in how you treat guests. You will profit more on relatability than
just revenue" – Janna Cachola

In addition, to relevance, when figuring out who to follow, it's important to evaluate relatability. Relatability, much like relevance, is a highly personal measure and addresses the question, "Am I able to connect to what the leaders, cause or objectives are offering or who they are?"

Those connections include our sense of self, our mission in life, development spiritually, mentally and physically and over-all well-being. Relatability is also a sense that the person who is leading identifies with who you are and where you are going in life.

As I have observed, in spite of a desire for connectedness with leaders, the reality is that while a leader may share your values, they may not always be relatable—especially when leadership's motives don't align with yours and when cultural context becomes a factor.

I am reminded of a very charismatic leader who I admired but could not pursue a mentorship with because I simply could not relate to him. Though I knew he had a lot of wisdom to offer, I understood that because I could not relate to him, I would not be able to grasp much of this wisdom. There was no connection, no hook.

On the other hand, in 2017, I discovered Patrick Bet David on YouTube, a charismatic Iranian American with an accent but with very practical information on entrepreneurship that I could relate to. I got hooked on his YouTube channel because I found his story, immigrant background, business examples and entrepreneurial discussion very relatable.

Being relatable cuts across many fields, we see this need for relatability within church settings. Congregants are often attracted to that young up and coming preacher with the high-top fade, skinny jeans and energetic delivery because congregants can relate to these pastors' stories and struggles. Relatability allows you to enter the same sphere as that which you are following.

Cultural context can play a big role in relatability. We previously talked about the GLOBE study, which sought to understand follower's perceptions of a leader relatability with cultural contexts.

The GLOBE study found that followers from high power distance countries were not really influenced by participatory leadership and could not really relate to leaders who exhibited that style[1]. Followers within this context were however drawn to leaders who were more authoritative and autocratic. So, culture can guide relatability. Certain leadership styles may hold no relatability and, therefore, may not allow a path to meaningful followership, because the cultural context does not work for the follower.

Let me say this at this point that there are always exceptions to the rules. For example, there are leaders who may not be relatable to you at first but become relatable over time especially when given a chance. Such leaders may end up growing on you as they say. In the same breath, there are leaders who may not be relatable at all but their relevance provides impetus for you to seek them out.

It is because of these possibilities that relatability is one of the more difficult aspects of choosing a leader to navigate. Relatability cannot therefore be the sole threshold used when choosing leaders.

Relatability is often linked to emotions and other intangible elements therefore, it is the easiest factor to manipulate. There are very few objective measures of relatability, so it is a hard factor to carefully assess. Simply put, you usually either feel relatability or you don't, it is in the eyes of the beholder so to speak. Armed with this knowledge, that relatability is often hard to objectively assess, corrosive leaders often focus on becoming relatable, so that they can manipulate people into followership relationships.

Therefore, though relatability can be an important aspect of healthy followership, it is prudent to ensure that relatability is not the factor you prioritize when determining who to follow.

CHAPTER SEVEN

The Respect Factor

"He who loves others is constantly loved by them. He who respects others is constantly respected by them" – Mencius

Aretha Franklin the late soul singer changed a generation with a seven-letter chorus lead in—R-E-S-P-E-C-T[1]. She pointed out the importance of respect, engaging audiences everywhere in evaluating the importance of respect. Similarly, our evaluation of whom we follow should include whether or not that individual respects. Specifically, does that leader have respect for God and other people?

To respect means to esteem, admire and think highly of someone, to show the importance of what others value and represent. While narcissistic leaders often influence their followers and demand forced respect, true leaders earn the respect of their followers by their actions.

The most significant action leaders who earn respect engage in is respect for their followers. A question followers must ask is whether or not there is mutual respect in the relationship. Specifically, a) is there respect for the office of the leader and for the person in the office, b) is there respect for the process and behavior of leadership? and c) does the leader respect followers?

Numerous sources speak to the importance of respect in healthy followership. In the Bible, we are told to respect and give honor to one another[2].

We see Jesus live out this philosophy in his leadership and followership. As he follows God, he shows a consistent deference to and respect for God. As he interacts with followers and the general public, Jesus consistently shows respect to people he encounters. Sometimes, Jesus explicitly accords respect to members of society that are shunned in his community, this endears his followers to Him. In an ultimate scene of respect, Jesus washes the feet of his disciples[3].

This example of respect fueled with humility, was one of the reasons I felt drawn to the message of the gospel. It guides my assessment of leaders. When I meet leaders, I observe how they treat their roles, how they behave when those who serve with them come around.

I look at their body language, facial expressions and overall authenticity when they interact with those around them. I am especially concerned with learning how leaders value others.

No group exemplifies the concept of respect than the military. I admire the military's work ethic and discipline. But, what I most admire is the respect that ebbs within the ranks. The military is built on a stringent concept of honor and respect. While this flows from the bottom to the top, it is always very refreshing to see it flow from the top to the bottom.

The Business Insider wrote an op-ed on General James "Mad Dog" Mattis. At the time, Mattis was the Secretary of Defense for the Trump administration. The article was unique in that it highlighted comments from General Mattis' subordinates. Most of the comments centered on Mattis' subordinates' perceptions of his leadership. One thing stood out, General Matthis was not just a leader who exemplified courage, dignity, decorum and intellect, he also demonstrated an immense respect for the people he led. Private Jack Manderville wrote the following about General Matthis:

"I have sat through multiple speeches given by senior officers. They are typically rife with platitudes and disingenuous praise. This was not one of those speeches. Mattis spoke like an enlisted man. He spoke to the enlisted man. He did this while keeping a gentlemanly manner about him.

In that speech, he sounded like an articulate warrior scholar as he sim-ultaneously praised us with unrepeatable expletives. He understood war. More importantly, he understood the people fighting it. We were the gener-ation that started calling him 'Mad Dog'"[4]

There is no better flattery than to hear a follower praise a leader for the respect they show to those who lead. Whether you agree or disagree with the General's views and past policies, the General's attitude proves that great leaders should ensure that respect flows both ways within the leadership follow-ership relationship. While there is a chance for false respect to exist – insincere respect, I think that followers must put on the respect radar, a gauge that looks into how leaders treat others.

When I was young, I observed how my father who was a sen-ior executive at an oil company treated his staff. I watched his reactions when they made mistakes, how he celebrated them when they performed well. Everyone was treated with dignity and respect. This behavior left an indelible mark on my mind and it was no wonder this staff enjoyed working with him. While some may argue otherwise, the respect factor is so im-portant in evaluating whom to follow.

CHAPTER EIGHT

The Result Factor

"Popularity is not leadership, results are" – Richie Norton

Followers must also evaluate the results of leadership they intend to follow or are following. There are varying levels to this evaluation because the result factor has multiple dimensions. Goran Swenson's work in the Total Quality Management magazine of 2005 explains some of these dimensions.

For instance, according to Swenson, a leader's performance or results must be looked at from a longitudinal perspective (over a time period) and within the specific context (business, non-profit or religious) in which the leadership followership relationship exists. People are more likely to follow individuals who have performed excellently over time in their fields of expertise as well as those who provide some form of psychological or spiritual impact on their lives[1].

For example, Oprah Winfrey was notorious for having what the media called at the time the "Oprah effect". Whenever Oprah endorsed, adhered to or promoted an idea, product or person, that idea product or person immediately saw a boost in the public's perception and followership. This resulted in increased sales or adherence to these ideas, products and people. This was possible because Oprah was known to deliver results. Warren Buffet one of the richest men in the world, has a reputation for picking value stocks due to a lifetime of effective results in the area of stock acquisition. So consistency in producing positive results is a key area in determining who to follow.

In addition to evaluating the results of leaders, followers must examine the leaders' behavior that leads to results. What this means is that it is important that the behaviors that lead to positive results are also acceptable. For an extreme example, we can look at autocratic leadership in general and say an autocratic leader, in particular claims to have dramatically reduced drug addiction rates in his country. Further inspection demonstrates that these questionable results, if they are even true, are the result of him murdering anyone suspected of using drugs.

In this case, the fact that the leader has garnered "results" is completely undermined by the behavior the leader is reflecting in getting those results.

Many examples abound of followers who engaged followership based on just a surface level assessment of the results produced by leaders, only to be disappointed.

On the other hand, in today's social media driven world, the strength of influence and result effectiveness is measured by the number of likes on Facebook or followers on Twitter and Instagram. This type of assessment alone would exclude followership of potentially great leaders who simply have not devoted time to building a social media presence. Secondly, this type of results assessments ignores the fact that a thriving social media following does not necessarily mean the leader is promoting anything worth following. Social media is rife with numerous personalities who do promote ideas that have no value to millions of people. However, if you are seeking a leader to teach you how to build a social media presence, then the leader's number of likes and followers would be paramount to assessing that leader's results.

Again, we find that context matters. Therefore, it is imperative that when evaluating results, the metrics being used to assess results are truly measures of the results required.

Many times other people's assessment of a leaders results may influence whether or not we follow well especially when the perceptions of a leader's results are made public. While it is important to gauge your analysis of a leader's results against other people, the public's assessment should be considered in line with your thoughtful analysis.

In the scriptures, we see an example of how the public perception of a leader's results impacted how that leader was followed. For years, King Saul was lauded for his prowess in battle and for being the ideal specimen of a true King. However, once David comes on the scene, the public determines that Saul's results are not as commendable.

In 1 Samuel 18:7, the Israelites sang, *"Saul has killed his thousands, and David his tens of thousands"* after David successfully killed Goliath. What does it mean that Saul has only killed thousands? Is that the result that is needed from your leader? Does your leader actually have to metaphorically kill tens of thousands for him to have results? That's why in order to follow well, you would have to carefully break apart this assessment of results to determine whether they're meaningful to you or your context.

What one forgets is that Saul gave David the platform to operate in the first place, we could also argue that by allowing David to step in the role of deliverer, King Saul was simply doing whatever was needed to win the battle given the circumstance however, that was not necessarily the way Israel viewed his contribution and subsequent results.

That is the same debate Basketball fans have when it comes to identifying who the greatest of all time (G.O.A.T) is in basketball. Many conclude that Michael Jordan is the G.O.A.T while others say that Lebron James is slowly taking that space. The argument against Lebron is that he does not have as many championship victories as Jordan.

So in this case, the question is, should we conclude that Lebron James is less of a leader, influencer or NBA player than Michael Jordan because he has less championship victories? There lies the dilemma with evaluating results. These in depth questions form a basis for our evaluations.

Another important thing to note is how leaders interpret the responses of the public to their results as well as how they respond to follower perceptions of needed results. Some leaders get very defensive or offended when the perceptions of the impact of their results is low. This was no more evident in the build up to the last presidential election on November 3rd 2020.

The entire mandate was determined by the citizen's perception on how President Trump handled racial tensions, white supremacy and most importantly the COVID-19 pandemic. As perceptions of the way the President handled the pandemic oscillated between admiration and disdain, President Trump's frustrations became evident from his tweets and responses which led to further alienation.

Similarly, this was the case with King Saul whose interpretation of the accolades directed towards David, resulted in jealousy and hatred for David.

David on the other hand when faced with similar predicament later in life, when public perception of Absalom his rebellious son was greater than his, prayed for his son Absalom. David was not bitter or defensive because he understood that a follower's perception of a leaders results is much more important than their actual numbers or results.

So to conclude, to follow well, we must exercise discernment in evaluating the results of a leader. It is not all about the numbers alone, the integrity of how those results were obtained and the spirit with which a leader conducts themselves in light of the public's perception of results are also vital.

So this brings us to the end of our consideration of the Four Rs of determining whom to follow—relevance, relatability, respect and results. Just as a careful consideration of these factors are important when choosing whom to follow, the Three Cs we will explore in the coming chapters—character, commitment and conviction—are also important.

CHAPTER NINE

The Character Factor

"To follow Christ is to become more like Him. It is to learn from His character" – Dieter F. Uchtdorf

C haracter refers to the distinct mental and moral qualities of an individual. Character is a definer that reflects who we are essentially. The scripture verse "we shall know them by their fruits (Matthew 7:20)," explains that the character of an individual can be ascertained by reviewing their fruits—the behaviors these individuals exhibit or the outcomes they achieve.

A very popular definition of character is one by James Hilman who stated that "character refers to deep structures of personality that are particularly resistant to change.[1]" With this in mind, a pivotal aspect of following well and investigating who to follow, is to look critically at a leader's character.

According to Larry C. Spear, a proponent of servant leadership "much of the leadership literature includes as an implicit assumption or belief that positive characteristics can, and should be, encouraged and practiced by leaders" (p.26)[2].

Spears further observed that aspects of a leader's character such as engaged listening, empathy, good stewardship, commitment to others' growth and foresight contribute to the overall growth of followers and encourages effective followership.

Examining these aspects of a leader's character can help you determine when authentic following of this leader is possible.

Sometimes, followers often fail to examine the character of the leader especially in times when an organization is just starting or when they are very successful. These extreme situations could blind side a follower and prevent effective evaluation of character. For instance, when an organization is just starting out and has not yet made a big mark, potential followers being excited about the new startup and all the imagery of future glory may overlook evaluating the character of these leaders. Sometimes it is hard for followers to take time to review character traits especially when deadlines are eminent and projects are worked on. Generally, the joy of building the organization may override any sense of objectivity towards character evaluation.

The same could be applicable when organizations are highly successful. Followers in this scenario may jump into a followership turning a blind eye and never examining a leader's character just because of the numbers and results obtained by the leadership as mentioned earlier. Followers stay on being complacent under bad leadership with unethical characteristics. It is only when the company is imploding that the general public finally becomes aware that leaders in the company were not guided by ethics, empathy or a concern for the public.

Enron was lauded as an industry leader in the 1990s but by 2001, it became clear that followers in the company were not engaged in a healthy followership. Many of the leaders were sustaining the company's success through criminal acts and would end up serving jail sentences for their behavior. Ongoing character evaluation of leaders would have been helpful.

The reality is that no leader is perfect, however, healthy followership can occur despite a leaders' flaws. That is why it is important that a leader's flaws do not directly contradict the mission of the organization, the health of the organization and your personal values and that a leader is actively engaged in personal growth—assessing and addressing his, hers or its flaws.

Having said that, leaders can deliberately hide their flaws. Therefore, it's imperative that followers remain vigilant and consistently assess leaders' characters.

Paul admonished a young Titus in Titus 2:2 to encourage the older men to display good character with judgment, faith, love and endurance. The implication of this is that no matter how long a leader has been in leadership, exhibiting good character remains fundamental to their acceptance by followers no matter the area, field or context.

This effect was in play once again in the 2020 presidential election. I think it is safe to say that the 2020 presidential election was to an extent a referendum on presidential character. Several polls taken during the election reflected that the perception of the president's character influenced the choice of who citizens voted for. Character evaluation must be matched with competency and results.

In conclusion, key character components to assess include integrity, courage, empathy, vision, and trustworthiness, emotional and spiritual intelligence. As followers review all of these attributes before choosing whom to follow, they will become increasingly savvy at selecting leaders they choose to follow.

CHAPTER TEN

The Commitment Factor

"Unless commitment is made there are only promises and hopes no plans" – Peter F. Drucker

C ommitment refers to the level of dedication a leader shows to the followers or cause. Commitment shows that the leaders care enough to invest time and energy into the calling, the people, mission or overall goal.

Followers should carefully review a leader's commitment, because commitment makes it more likely that the leader will be an effective influence in your life. Leaders demonstrate their commitment through the amount of time, money and sweat they are willing to invest in the cause and followers.

We see commitment in Jesus' leadership (and followership). Jesus invests a considerable amount of time to be with his disciples and to care for them and the general public.

Specifically, he spent a lot of time and effort praying for them, teaching them, and comforting them. Ultimately, His commitment is shown in his willingness to die for them. Even on the negative side, bad leaders are followed because of their commitment even though they may promote bad values.

There is something very attractive about someone who is committed. If you want to know who to follow, look at their commitment levels. How committed are the leaders to what they are promoting?

Does this commitment waiver over time? Does this commitment change in times of stress and difficulty? On the other hand, commitment could be transactional in other words, leaders can project a false sense of commitment to you because of the expectation of outcomes or because of something they want to get out of the relationship.

So it's not just evaluating the level of commitment from a surface level but also evaluating the leader's motivations for showing commitment which may be shellfish and negative.

A theory that explains organizational commitment is Becker's (1960) side-bet theory, which states that organizational commitments increase with the accumulation of side bets or investments[1]. In essence, the more investments made towards a follower the less likely the follower jumps ship because of the perception that they would miss out on these investments if they do leave. The reality is that the level of investments or commitments is a function of several factors which includes the type and productivity of the follower as well as the way a leader views vision, participation and overall acceptance in light of the follower. Although, evaluating the commitment of those we follow is a complex process, we can approach the process by gauging some leadership behaviors.

Below are some broad conceptual categories that define varying commitment styles of leaders based on the leader's view of vision, participation and overall acceptance of the follower's role or place in fulfilling the leaders overall goals.

Star Gazers

The star gazers are visionary leaders who are often looking at the stars and not the streets metaphorically. These leaders love new things and are often innovative and driven by images of the future. They are always intrigued by the new team member, new employer and love the new follower that they perceive will add value to their team. They get bored with the status quo very quickly and any follower that falls within that box of status quo. Star gazers' commitment level shifts rapidly as ideas and followers lose their novelty.

They love to change things up every month or so leaving those who work with them confused about projects that they just started but not completed. They are very trusting of new people, new technology, and always ready to give individuals a chance to advance the vision. Vision is not static, but dynamic, with the star gazer. Their motivation is the vision, the stars and the end goals.

Therefore, these leaders' greatest strength and weakness is their ability to hone in and fully commit to new people, projects and missions, sometimes at the expense of followers who have been with them for a while.

In the long term, followers who have been with these leaders for a while, may feel left behind by these types of leaders. Followers of a star gazer may also never experience true forward motion, if these leaders search for the new and exciting, leads a trail of unfinished projects.

Street Walkers

Street walkers are strong leaders who are focused on keeping things running smoothly on the ground. Unlike the Star gazers, their eyes are not so much on what is ahead but on what is on the ground. Street walkers provide a day to day managerial grind that is focused on keeping the ship running. They are focused on maintenance and rarely innovation. Therefore, their favorite moto is that "If it ain't broke, don't fix it."

They love to get their hands dirty and are chronic microman-agers, enjoying the minutia of daily operations. Street walkers love the status quo and allow very few modifications.

They love to reminisce about the past and tout their past glo-ries. Street walkers don't trust easily, you have to win their trust over time. They are committed and dedicated to those who over time have proven their loyalty and are not very trust-ing of new followers.

They are extremely suspicious and paranoid about their po-sition being usurped because they keep their nose to the ground. Vision is static and they are bound by the letter of the law. Their motivation is the street's perception of them not nec-essarily their vision of tomorrow.

They are committed to those who have been committed to the cause over a long period of time. Thus, new followers often feel left on the outside. They may be ignored or omitted from critical decision making tasks because they have not earned their stripes.

Sky Scrappers

These are larger than life personalities who are extremely loyal to those who are loyal to them. They combine some of the traits of the star gazers and street walkers and have the ad-vantage of seeing the sky but also have the ability to connect to the streets. They are scrappy and love a good fight. They know how to relate but may not be diplomatic due to their larger than life personalities.

They both delegate and micro-manage. They are sometimes very erratic and often leave their followers wondering where they fit. Because they are motivated by the size of their influence and personality, they are sometimes perceived as insensitive. They love those who admire them and invest in those who shower them with praise and appreciation.

They value loyalty, so followers who do not toe the line, rarely feel the fullness of skyscrapers' commitment. This type of leader entices followers who are attracted to their larger than life personality and influence. These leaders tend to be tenacious and lead with great focus.

Stream Swimmers

These are leaders who roll with the punches so to speak. They have learnt through adversity and challenges to survive and have carved out a niche for themselves. They love all comers, new, old, it doesn't matter, but their commitment is to those who show expertise. They value skills and flexibility and are attracted to followers who have this trait. They invest in followers that demonstrate their usefulness. Stream swimmers are leaders that know how to swim in the midst of an undercurrent and have no patience for those who cannot pick themselves up from adversity.

Vision is also dynamic with them, it is not static but constantly changing. They are also innovative and love problems solvers. Followers who love to solve problems are attracted to these Stream Swimmers. Their level of commitment is based on adaptability and transparency.

A review of these different leadership categories demonstrates that as followers investigate potential leader's commitment, it is important to understand the leader's style. A leader's commitment style can directly affect the level of commitment that leader will have towards their followers. Since a leader's commitment to you is an integral part of healthy followership, it is very important to be able to approximate what the leader's initial commitment to you would be and to understand what fluctuations, if any, would occur in that commitment level and adjust accordingly.

Omokhai Imoukhuede Ph.D.

CHAPTER ELEVEN

The Conviction Factor

*"A man of conviction is often more to be desired than
a man of experience" – Curt Siodmak*

Conviction reflects a fixed or firm belief in something. Leaders with conviction often inspire followership because it uncovers their resolve about what they are projecting. Since alignment with a leader's ideals is a key part of deciding who to follow, it is important for followers to assess leaders' conviction to those expressed ideals.

I remember a school assignment to do a qualitative study on the speeches made by two American Presidents. The goal of the assignment was to transcribe two speeches each for each President and then code or summarize themes or points that stood out in their speeches. I picked President Ronald Regan and Barack Obama for my evaluations and was surprised at my findings.

From my coding, I found out that both presidents had some similarities in their professed ideals, in spite of their stark ideological differences. Both Presidents showed similar convictions in their values for pragmatism and optimism. In the selected speeches both presidents were hopeful about the future, but very pragmatic about existing challenges. Both presidents showed strong convictions for courage, service and sacrifice.

For example, President Obama showed strong conviction through his courage in running for office of the President in 2008, despite his limited experience on the federal level. President Reagan, on the other hand, showed his strong conviction through his courage in tackling communism. These convictions were reflected in their speeches. Additionally, both presidents showed strong dependence in their use of historical references and humor to communicate their agenda while also being open for dialogue and communication.

I think it was these passionate convictions and unwavering beliefs even in areas of political differences like the role of government that made these two leaders attractive to their followers. In understanding how to follow well, it is important to review what drives the convictions of those who lead. Examine the leaders' beliefs about life, their beliefs about others and the outcomes of the decisions guided by their beliefs.

For example, in a conversation, a friend of mine mentioned that he had a mentor whose convictions about other leaders in the ministry led the mentor to be extremely judgmental and condescending. The mentor truly believed that ministry could only thrive if you called out any minister you thought was wrong. Although the mentor meant well, his strong convictions and approach towards reprimanding other ministers was very brash.

My friend subsequently ended the relationship with the mentor because even though the mentor was sincere, his convictions guided him to act in a manner my friend felt was harmful. The mentor's convictions overruled any empathy towards those he was judgmental about. This example shows how followers examine the convictions of a leader to determine that their beliefs or convictions no longer align.

Much like many of the previous factors, there is a high level of subjectivity when it comes to these evaluations. As you evaluate the leaders' convictions, the yardstick will be your beliefs about what is good and what is bad mentioned earlier. Therefore, it is important to continue honing your base sense of morality and personal convictions so that you become more adept at wisely analyzing whether a leaders' convictions make them the appropriate person for you to follow.

Another way to evaluate convictions is to take time to study biographies and books if available by the leaders you intend to follow. These books give insights into the leader's stories, narratives and convictions. However caution must be taken in validating the sources of this information.

Other elements may make the evaluation of a leader's convictions difficult. Some leaders' may be deliberately trying to mislead the public and their followers. So watch to see if the person's professed beliefs match their actions.

If the professed beliefs are acceptable, but the leader's behavior is unacceptable, it is most likely that the behavior is a better indicator of the leader's true convictions. The actions and the focus of that leader, usually best reflect the leader's convictions or beliefs.

CHAPTER TWELVE

Understand Why We Follow

"We follow those who lead not because we have to but
because we want to" – Simon Sinek

I once attended a Microsoft sponsored conference and was intrigued by a common theme emphasized by the keynote speakers. Conference speakers explained that Microsoft's earlier business model was to emphasize the product or the technology over the actual need the product was meeting.

A change in strategy, from a focus on (the product) to a focus on the why (the need), gave users an opportunity to discuss needs and why they felt the technology is needed. So based on this, Microsoft stopped churning out software plagued with endless licenses and switched their model to a partnership led, subscription-based format that is solely built on the customer needs. Similarly, following well, needs an emphasis on the why.

Understanding why following is needed or important creates a context that better motivates us on our quest, allowing us to take steps towards our followership goals or objectives.

Understanding the reason, the why, for anything helps to bring out the value of and points to the purpose of the understood thing. In the book, *Start with Why, How Great Leaders Inspire Everyone to Take Action*, Simon Sinek explained that addressing the importance of knowing the why behind anything helps us locate our awareness of the significance or importance of what we are pursuing[1].

This understanding is the strategy technology organizations like Microsoft are using to increase market value, build partnerships and grow business profit. There are certain dynamics where followership occurs organically and implicitly due to a leader's character, traits and behaviors as discussed earlier, however, there are other conceptual factors occurring within the follower that influence how followers perceive a leader which results in why followers follow. They are:

Fear

Fear is a powerful psychological occurrence that impacts leadership and followership relationships.

In the great and "dirty" battle for Stalingrad between Germany and Russia during the Second World War, the Russian army was at a crossroads. The German army was advancing rapidly as they swiftly obliterated everything in their path leading up to that fight.

Stalin, realizing that Stalingrad was probably the last point of resistance to the German army, utilized scare tactics on his people. His orders were that his citizens stand up and fight or risk losing their entire nation. These poor citizens were so full of fear of loss that they threw themselves into the trenches to fight.

Fear in this case was the motivation to follow which resulted in the defeat of Germany in what historians call the bloodiest battle in the history of warfare at the time. Although the outcome worked in favor of the Russians in this case, this is not always the case. The Enron example provided earlier, is a case of fear-based followership, where accountants for fear of losing their jobs engaged in unethical acts perpetrated by flawed leadership[2].

The purpose of discussing this example is not to advocate the use of fear in leadership but to simply state that it can be a tool utilized to garner individuals to follow.

The fear factor is a reason why people follow, the fear of failure, the fear of the unknown, and in the case of the Russians in Stalingrad, the fear of loss.

Although fear is a powerful motivator for following, it is not the best and should be resisted if possible. Jody Gittel in an MIT Sloan review stated that while fear could motivate followership in the short run, it usually backfires and recommended that establishing a strong positive relationship is better to influence high performance than fear[3].

Fear in followership breeds silence, many abused victims have subjected their wills because of fear. Victims are bound by the perception of shame and cower in fear of judgment. Followers must develop courage to face this why, confront the fears and speak up if need be when it is determined that your followership is fear based.

Familiarity

Familiarity means close acquaintance or knowledge of something. The more you are familiar, the more comfortable you are with who you plan to follow. Also, the more familiar you perceive your leader to be with you as a follower, the more you follow them. When followers perceive that their values align with their leaders, it breeds some form of familiarity and connectedness.

I am more likely to allow someone to influence me when there is some level of familiarity either through value alignment or simply a deep sense of communication. Familiarity is an important component and predictor for behavioral change in followers and the greater the familiarity with leadership through interaction, the more likely followers learn and apply leadership techniques[2].

All these points to a reason why we follow, in as much as following as mentioned earlier, is a function of our wills, it is also in essence a function of trust and familiarity increases trust. There is a comfort level that exists when one is familiar with a goal, vision, or even a leader. This means that for this bond of familiarity to get stronger, constant communication is required.

The point I am making here is that people follow individuals who have figured out a way to bring down the walls to create intimacy with those they influence because intimacy is a result of familiarity as well.

While one can argue that familiarity can bring contempt, this is not empirically proven though, howbeit conceptually received. The reality is that individuals are more likely to follow ideals, ideas, and leaders who through transparency and authenticity create an environment for familiarity either directly or indirectly.

Finance

A study was done on the profiles of suicide bombers. One common thing found in their profile was that they came from very poor backgrounds[4]. These individuals, it seemed, joined extremist groups because of the promise of a better financial life for their families and friends.

The same is true for gang members in inner cities or members of the mafia, who are enticed by the expensive lifestyles of drug dealers as they hope to find freedom from poverty and lack.

The belief that one's economic conditions can change for the better influences the desire to follow especially when it comes to finances. The impact of financial pressure is seen in everyday life as well, as people work in jobs they do not necessarily like to improve their financial status.

While making the decision to follow based on finances alone may yield both positive and negative results, it is worth noting that our quest to follow based on finances must be matched with our underlining values.

Finance is a very strong reason individuals follow especially when there is a lack of it, and to follow well, we have to evaluate to what extent following based on finances crosses the line beyond our values for living in love which is ultimately the essence of followership.

Fun

Individuals follow for fun. This is a known fact as the number of subscribers for apps related to sports, music, or even religion continues to increase and increase. People love to have fun and anything that stirs up that emotion will garner followership.

The fun factor is real and must not be ignored. Many individuals unfortunately spend countless hours online because of the fun they derive from such activities.

It is safe to say that you can get a crowd together under the guise of having fun than any other thing. I am constantly reminded of this with my young children. Whenever I exclude fun from an assigned task, I get pushback or complaints from them. However, once fun is injected, a different type of response ensues. Anything that provides amusement or enjoyment creates an incentive for followership.

In essence, anything that is fun to us creates a sense of belonging, it triggers a satisfaction that keeps us moving in the direction and influence of the source of that fun. This sense of love and belonging often plays out in a motivation to follow.

Food

Individuals follow when they sense that they will obtain nourishment from those who lead them. In this case, food is a metaphor for investments from leaders that provide some form of nourishment that followers feel they would lose if they did not follow.

In John 6:26 Jesus answered, *"Very truly I tell you, you are looking for me, not because you saw the signs I performed but because you ate the loaves and had your fill."*

This is interesting because Jesus saw through the inquiry of the crowd and concluded that there was a self-serving reason they were looking for him and that it was primarily because of the food they received from him.

People will travel thousands of miles, cross even deserts to be able to have food on their table. Investment of food which can also be a metaphor for income as well, reflects a very important reason why people are committed and why they follow.

Following as we see, provides a way to meet our basic needs, the hunter-gatherers would leave their settlements, following tracks in search for food and nourishments.

The more the perception of a leader who can provide such nourishments, the more committed that follower consistently pursues.

Faith

In John 6:35 Jesus declared, "*I am the bread of life. Whoever comes to me will never go hungry, and whoever believes in me will never be thirsty.*" The substitution of a reason to follow from just physical nourishment to strong belief reflects a fundamental reason why people follow. The ability to believe is what separates us from animals. The reality is that faith is a choice that affects our wills to trust in who is leading us even when it seems like there is no hope.

When I examine employees especially within startups, I see a motivation to join a cause purely from a standpoint of faith. Many times, these individuals do not have the money or connections to advance the cause but just simply have faith, availability and enthusiasm that what they are doing will work.

Following based on faith especially when the causes are noble, is one of the most rewarding things that can happen to an individual.

The reality though is that it may not always be fun at the beginning but in the end, it pays off. Abraham's story in the Bible re-enforces this. Abraham is a seventy-five-year-old man with a barren wife. He has this dream and leaves the comfort of his family with his wife and belongings on a followership quest.

Ten years in, he has still not experienced his dream and is looking for reassurance from God about the fulfillment of his dream. It was faith in God that kept Abraham and his wife going. After 25 years of literally wandering around, Abraham and Sarah's dream was fulfilled, they have a son and find a place to settle. Their followership why was simply their faith.

CHAPTER THIRTEEN

Understanding True Followership

"Followership does not mean changing the rank of followers but changing their response to their rank, their response to their superiors, and the situation at hand."— Barbara Kellerman

Followership can be good or bad. This means we can follow correctly or incorrectly. Also, followers can exhibit certain qualities or behaviors or may engage in processes that could yield negative or positive followership outcomes. To follow well, we must come to an authentic understanding of what true followership is not. Here are some misconceptions of true followership.

True followership is not the loss of your identity

No two fingerprints are alike; we all have our individual personalities. Though we were created to live relationally, connect communally and learn from one another, we still possess our individuality. The Bible states that we are wonderfully and fear-fully made[1], meaning that each person possesses unique qualities and behaviors that make us special. These unique qualities are important influencers in what we choose to follow. Therefore, without a retention of this uniqueness and individuality there is no true followership, because there is no true choice.

True followership is not just copying or mimicking someone. It does not command the loss of your identity. Rather, true followership utilizes your individuality to connect you to something greater than yourself. For instance, building materials are put together to form a home. For the house to stand, it is crucial for all of the pieces to remain connected together. But, these pieces must also retain their individual identity. For example, light fixtures must remain physically connected to the ceiling in the intended room. But, it is also equally important that these fixtures retain their identities as fixtures. They would be useless if they suddenly morphed and became a concrete ceiling. Likewise, once they rust and disintegrate, they are no longer useful members of the home.

Therefore, calls to true, healthy followership will demand that, as you adhere to the group's context, regulations and/or purpose, that you remain an individual.

Followership may lead you to change aspects of yourself, but will never require that you completely abandon who you are.

For instance, followership may lead you to adopt virtues that you admire in a person, to become less selfish, or to spend more time working on the goal. However, as you make these adjustments, there should be a unique way that you go about this work that allows you to retain a sense of self.

This continual effort to retain a sense of self as you follow is not a self-centered approach. It is actually based on an understanding that you are uniquely equipped to impact the world. God has individualized us because there are very specific, individual problems in this world that each of us is uniquely equipped to resolve.

Therefore, the best thing you can do for the world at large, is for you to be all that God has called you to be. Living at any level less than who you are, limits your contributions to the growth and success of those around you. One of the reasons many followers, especially within the church context, get burned out or frustrated is because they believe true followership is losing oneself to those they follow within the church. In this extreme scenario, the people forget their families, relinquish healthy activities that gave them pleasure or contributed to their wellness—all in the name of being a follower. Relinquishing these aspects of their "self" quickly makes their followership hollow. The only person to lose ourselves is God and even when that occurs, God promises that you will find your true self in the process[2].

You see, one of the elements of emotional intelligence is self-awareness; the same is also true for authentic followership. Emotionally intelligent, authentic followers are very aware of their social setting as well as their sense of self. Authentic followers do not have a complex when it comes to their weaknesses and strengths[3]. They are in tune with this aspect of their lives. Therefore, their followership leads them to self-discovery and originality.

One of the first things my pastor told me when we met was that he wanted to be a mat for me to step on to achieve my calling and destiny. I had never heard anything like that before. It is only in recent years, armed with my knowledge of followership, that I can fully appreciate that statement. That statement reflected a selfless leader who was willing to sacrifice his time, energy, finances, wisdom so that those who followed grew to be the best of themselves. The statement not only reflected selflessness on the leader's part but humility and security in the leader's self-worth. Selfless leaders attract selfless and self-aware followers.

The goal of followership is self-actualization through transcendent actions.

For example, through their association with Jesus Christ, the disciples reflected Christ like abilities. They began to carry out similar miracles. But, we see that they still retained their sense of self. Peter, for instance, still had a thick Galilean accent, you can see his individuality in his writings and things written about him in the Bible. As a follower, Peter could preach the true gospel, but he was doing it in his own style and manner. He did give up some of the narrow thoughts he had on the person of the Messiah. However, he came to this understanding and reflected this truth in his own way and time.

Thus, true followership prompts the follower to find themselves as they give themselves to followership. While one may not be able to avoid copying skills and mannerism of an admired mentor, the goal of true followership is to get to the point where you develop who you truly are.

The late Kobe Bryant's relationship with Michael Jordan expresses this. The young Kobe Bryant was so focused on being like Mike that he talked, walked, and approached the game of basketball like Michael Jordan. Kobe soaked up every detail about Michael and tried to imitate it. This led Kobe to be a good player.

Eventually, Kobe began to emerge as a great player as his style began to change and lean on his uniqueness. Kobe was able to stand out amongst his peers, creating his own legacy even though he acknowledged the influence of Michael Jordan.

Another example of true followership inspiring individuality can be found in the Bible. David grew up seeing King Saul as the model of a warrior and a king.

There came a time when Israel was faced with war against their sworn enemy the Philistines and had been challenged for days by the Philistine champion, Goliath. David sees himself as a follower of the King and in the King and Israel's name, he persuades King Saul to allow him to fight Goliath. Before the battle Saul offers his armor to David. David humbly refuses to use the armor. David explains that he has not fought with armor before.

Additionally, the armor was too big for David. David then goes on to face the Goliath using his own style of fighting and is successful. Therefore, David's followership only yields positive results because David follows within his uniqueness instead of trying to follow in imitation of the king. David had not proved the armor Saul presented to him. True followership provides an opportunity for us to be comfortable in our own skin utilizing our unique gifts and calls. So there you have it, followership is indeed not a loss of your identity.

True followership is not static.

Many erroneously advance the view that followership requires stagnation. Adherents to this misconception believe that followership prohibits motion, because it requires you to remain allegiant to a single spot, to a single cause.

This is incorrect. True followership results in the development and growth of the follower. When we look at Jesus' disciples we see the growth experienced by each. The disciples were a bunch of men and women who were often outcasts or within the lowest rungs of society.

They had many misconceptions; some glorified violence, others embraced the oppressive societal and religious structures that excluded them from the mainstream. As they followed, though, we see that their followership leads them in a process of spiritual growth and development.

When you follow well, there is a reciprocal nourishment within the leader/follower relationship that produces motivation for both the leaders and followers. Therefore, true followership is not static, there is progression and movement, motivation and advancement.

When we follow correctly, by choosing the right leaders and causes, we experience this motivation to be better.

We experience growth. God created us with abilities that enable self-growth which occurs for the benefit of others. True followership results in the development and growth of the follower. For this to happen, followers must be cultivated, developed, groomed, and invested in to bring out the best in the cause. One of the roles of leadership is that they are responsible for grooming, training, and empowering those who follow them. True followership is established when this aspect is fulfilled in the lives of the follower regardless of the rank, role, process, or behavior exhibited by the follower. I can trace the development of several aspects of my life to this knowledge that I must be making progress as I engage followership.

In my earlier years of following, I struggled with my communication with my leaders, I always wanted to be right about whatever ideas I had at the time and this rubbed my leaders the wrong way at times. In all honesty, being self-aware, I knew I could do better, so I willingly accepted the process of change and with the help of my leader, I began to work on this area of my followership. Not too long after, I made progress in this area. No matter the area, following well occurs in an atmosphere of humility, grace and love from both the leaders and followers and when this exists you will experience movement as a mark of true followership.

True followership is not forced servitude

There is a misconception that followers are weak, unmotivated and lack critical thinking abilities[4]. In reality, true followers play as important a role in the success of the organization as leaders do. These perceptions are what fuels the stigma associated with the word "follower."

There has to be a renewal of our perception of followership. We need to see true followership as something that is not forced or inspired by fear, but, rather, something that is earned and ultimately liberating. True followers carefully examine and should only follow after that examination proves that the leader is worthy of followership. Even in the process of following, we must not feel obligated to remain in a leader-follower relationship that is negative or detrimental to one's emotional or professional growth as discussed earlier.

I have heard several disturbing stories of followers who feel trapped in their leader-follower relationships who do not feel empowered to have their voices heard. While there are situations where followers may prefer to have more autocratic leadership, true followership entails that followers must have a voice, a place at the table and freedom to be the best of themselves.

CHAPTER FOURTEEN

Followership Disappointments, Faith and Cost

"You need to keep your emotions in balance, treading that fine line between commitment to your goals and disappointment when they do not come to fruition, whilst still being optimistic and positive about the future" —Tom Laurie

Followership opens you to the risk of disappointment. I have watched people languish in the agony of the disappointment from broken expectations. Followers sometimes struggle to recover when their leaders fall from grace. The hurt is real and the disappointment true.

So, we must approach followership with the understanding that though we can diminish the likelihood of falling under bad leaders by adhering to all the earlier mentioned principles, we may not be able to completely eliminate that possibility.

Therefore, it is important to continue to review leaders as we follow, so that we can quickly respond to indications that there are problems within the leadership-followership relationship. Each problem will require different solutions—ranging from a discussion with the leader to one of the most drastic solutions, leaving the followership and alerting others of the danger of following this leader. It will require courage to address the uncomfortable environment within the leadership–followership relationship and prayers to maintain focus on your ultimate goal.

As you follow, it is important to remember that followership hinges on you—your individuality, your desires, your discernment, your calling and in dealing with the disappointments, we have to accept that leaders are human and capable of making mistakes hence a need for evaluating the leader in light of our values, from a stand point of love and in objective prayers.

So work to ensure that as you follow, you maintain a healthy sense of your self-worth this is where it begins. Making the correct decision when you realize there are problems with following will often hinge on your sense of self-worth which is linked to your values and the God factor. Many times when toxic leadership is encouraged and allowed to persist, it is usually because those following have to yet come to terms with who they are, their sense of self-worth and values of love and respect. When this is not in place, followers become complacent in bad leadership.

One of my favorite speeches by Martin Luther King Jr, was a speech titled *"What is your life's Blueprint?"* In that 1967 speech, Martin Luther King Jr addressing students from Barratt High School in Philadelphia said, *"number one in your life's blueprint should be a deep belief in your own dignity, your own worth and your own some-bodiness, don't allow anybody to make you feel that you are nobody..."*

Dr King Jr's speech reflected that embracing one's sense of appreciation for their race and identity in light of the oppressive segregated society of 60's America, was essential for not only building a successful life but also for pushing back against any form of oppressive leadership, system or ideal. A healthy sense of self creates authenticity in approaching disappointments in leadership-followership relationships. It also prevents us from being so critical about leaders especially when we have percep-tions that they are supposed to be perfect. Therefore, we must be ready to get a balanced perspective about the leader's behav-ior, personality, decisions and choices. Getting a fresh perspec-tive of your current leadership-followership space helps when conducted through the lens of love and grace. This will help you to be objective yet empathetic, forgiving yet practical and pa-tient yet courageous as you decide on your next steps.

You must also realize that to deal with disappointments in followership, you have to differentiate between personal leadership errors and process leadership errors. Personal leadership errors occur due to leadership character flaws like insecurities, low self-esteem, lack of integrity, narcissistic attitudes etc that affects a followers sense of self, values and trust. Process leadership errors on the other hand, are errors that relate to how a leader or organization likes things done within their system and how these processes affect the overall performance of the followers. Followers must take time to evaluate the impact of both errors on their overall followership goals, missions and objectives. Ultimately the level of disappointment will be determined by the leader's willingness to address such errors and their inclination to make adequate changes when needed.

Faith and Followership

My personal journey of followership continues and remains full of life lessons but, by and large, followership has led to fulfillment in my life, my calling and my relationship with Christ. I initially stumbled into followership, not really knowing what it was.

In my early years of followership discovery, there were no seminars or self-help books focused on followership. The Bible, therefore, was the only thing nudging me towards developing an understanding of true followership. Unbeknown to me, these Biblical values of followership were etched in my consciousness, providing a compass that led to this quest. Followership, ultimately, is faith, it is faith in what is leading you, faith in who is leading, faith that somehow everything will work out.

One of the first challenges I faced with followership was as a young adult. I was at a crossroad, deciding whether or not to drop out of engineering school. After some self-reflection, I realized that studying engineering was not for me. I only pursued that path because I felt the tremendous pressure to measure up to friends and some family members who were actually engineers. So instead of following what reflected my strengths, passions and what I loved, cherished and valued, I pushed those desires to the side out of fear and pressure and just basically struggled for two years in engineering school.

However, at some point, I had to come to terms with this drive to engage my true passions. Even as I clung to the mentorship of family members who were successful engineers, I could not shake my true desire and God prompting to move to a different field. So, I began a month of prayer, seeking God's wisdom at this time. I unconsciously went through the steps prescribed in this book, asking questions about my values, self-worth and what role engineering played in my life.

After that month I was sure. In a moment of clarity, I called my friends and my brothers who were in the same college and explained that I was dropping out of engineering school. The next morning I left the school and embarked on a three hour bus ride home. Each mile of the journey, I sat in trepidation, worried about how my parents would react.

I left the comfort of what seemed the obvious followership path—a team of mentors in engineering and admission to an engineering school—to follow what felt like a God prompting. As I surrendered, opportunities arose. Within three weeks I was accepted into a school program that allowed me to study international business. My parents came around as they saw the authenticity of my followership. Within a few months, I was on my way to Spain, not knowing a word of Spanish, but firmly on my way towards my true path.

Understanding and applying followership opens you to adventures. True followership will often present challenges and unfamiliar settings that mold and build you. I cannot recount all of the lessons I learned in Madrid—it was a time of unprecedented personal growth in my youth. By the time I completed my international business degree, I graduated at the top of my class and transitioned into a fulfilling career path. I never considered engineering again once I dropped out of the school.

Inauthentic followership would have convinced me to remain under the mentorship of leaders guiding me towards goals that did not correspond with my inner promptings. Therefore, my entire life is owed to the fact that God helped me identify that I was on the wrong followership path. I had to believe that my steps were in the right direction and that my path though different would lead to a destination of fulfilment.

Cost of Followership

Despite being on the correct followership path when I dropped out of engineering school, my journey was not without challenges and sacrifices. This ties in to the title of this chapter because the decision to move out of Nigeria cost me some friendships, a life of comfort and relieved me from an environment I was comfortable with to one where I had very little control. In my stay in Madrid, I experienced racism and suffered humiliation due to my immigration status in Spain. I was even tempted several times to doubt my faith.

Though I was on the right path, I still had to carry out the followership review each step of the way. As I evaluated whether my dream was worth following, I also had to find new mentors in foreign spaces. With each of these leaders, I had to examine the cost of my overall vision and review whether these mentorship relationships were worth following. Through this followership journey, I had to embrace and come to terms with my self-worth, the values and gifts I brought to the table.

In these new spaces, I let my leaders know what I struggled with in my one on one sessions, I expressed my concerns and was quick to celebrate areas of strength.

I volunteered to use my gifts and strength and voraciously worked on areas of weakness. I sought feedback and accepted feedback, eventually rebuilding a new support base of mentors and creating a healthy space where I could be myself yet focused on a vision.

Once I was in this healthy space, my followership could take on greater dimensions. I began to seek out ways to serve and, as a result, the Lord began to create opportunities on my followership path for me to serve others and positively impact their lives.

I have come to a point where I see the role followership plays in the grand scheme of things. It is not something I compartmentalize within a genre of social studies, but something that I see as the fabric for all human existence.

As a result of this, I am constantly evaluating my biases, refocusing my followership lens because the subject is broad and requires more study and focus. I am constantly conscious of the God factor, regularly evaluating my inner promptings for significance and how following reflects my overall motives juxta-posed with God. These realities have caused me to look at the bigger picture, thereby approaching life as though it is beyond my individual existence. Understanding followership to me means that the motives and end goals of my following well is service to those around me. Which means that if I am to serve others well, I must learn their context, I must participate in their stories to fully understand their existence. This was the mindset my wife and I had in 2013 when we moved to the Southside of Chicago to follow the vision laid by our local church to work with families and community within that neighborhood. It was a tough decision but at the end it paid off because we got to understand better the stories, experiences and existence of those we were called to reach. The same is applicable to those who embark on this journey.

I have used this same process of studying context to evaluate my work environment, to look at the leaders, the staff, culture and philosophy to help me determine the appropriate responses per time. I have to say that understanding followership has helped me discern, discern my place, my purpose, my potential, and my power.

Ultimately, true followership is a journey to discover in what way we were uniquely created to serve humanity. So let's take advantage of this knowledge and step into the fullness of yourself by becoming a true follower.

Conclusion

So to follow well, we must accept the importance followership plays in the grand scheme of things. We have to be open to the subject and put aside any biases or preconceived notions about followership.

To follow well, we have to recognize the God factor when it comes to followership as we recognize that followership is really about God and the inner promptings for significance and purpose. Our followership is really an expression for the greater one in our lives.

To follow well, we have to recognize the unique contexts and situations that the leadership/followership relationship exists so that we can apply appropriate responses to the correct context.

Followership occurs within a reciprocal relationship with leadership, so we have to have a criteria to choose who to follow. Leaders who are relevant, relatable, show respect and are result oriented, have good character, can communicate, show commitment and have strong convictions reflect factors that help us know who to follow.

To follow well we have to know why we follow, fear, familiarity, finance, food and fun are some reasons. We have to also know what true followership is not and deal with some misconceptions about followership.

Finally, following well may open us up for disappointments which we mitigate by acknowledging the flawed nature of everyone, asking questions and not taking things too personal. There is also cost when we follow and our hope is that we engage our followership with faith using the information from this book to help us conceptually follow so we can be all that God has for us.

ACKNOWLEDGEMENTS

This book would not be possible without God whose influence and inspiration kept motivating me to see this 10 year project to completion.

To my wife Osen and children Alina, Sophia, Hannah and Jeremiah-Stephen, you all make my life a joyful experience, thanks Osen for your love, support and inspiration throughout this project.

To Emi Aprekumah. my editor, thanks for pulling out the words I did not know how to communicate from me. Thanks for the excellent work on this project.

To my parents Stephen Obaseki and Roseline Imoukhuede, siblings Imohimi, Odion, Omoh, Imoghome and Emilomo, you created the space for me to examine followership earlier on, I would not be the man I am without you.

To my Pastors, Pastors Gregory Lan and Debo Ijiwola, thanks for your continued support and leadership example.

To my Church family and friends all over the world, thanks for your prayers and support.

Omokhai Imoukhuede Ph.D.

NOTES

Introduction

Quote: Riggio, R. E., Chaleff, I., & Lipman-Blumen, J. (Eds.). (2008). The art of followership: How great followers create great leaders and organizations (Vol. 146). John Wiley & Sons.

1. Kim, W. C., & Mauborgne, R. (2014). Blue ocean strategy, expanded edition: How to create uncontested market space and make the competition irrelevant. Harvard business review Press.

2. Riggio, R. E., Chaleff, I., & Lipman-Blumen, J. (Eds.). (2008). The art of followership: How great followers create great leaders and organizations (Vol. 146). John Wiley & Sons.

3. Kellerman, B. (2008). Followership: How followers are creating change and changing leaders: Harvard Business School Press Boston.

4. Riggio, R. E., Chaleff, I., & Lipman-Blumen, J. (Eds.). (2008). The art of followership: How great followers create great leaders and organizations (Vol. 146). John Wiley & Sons.

5. Imoukhuede, O. (2019). The Impact of Entrepreneurial Leadership on Authentic Followership in Nigeria and the United States (Doctoral dissertation, Regent University).

Chapter One

Quote retrieved from http://www.finestquotes.com/quote-id-5112.htm

1. Collinson, D. (2006). Rethinking followership: A post-structuralist analysis of follower identities. The Leadership Quarterly, 17(2), 179-189.

2. Kellerman, B. (2008). Followership: How followers are creating change and changing leaders: Harvard Business School Press Boston.

3. John 14:12

4. Uhl-Bien, M., Riggio, R. E., Lowe, K. B., & Carsten, M. K. (2014). Followership theory: A review and research agenda. The Leadership Quarterly, 25(1), 83-104.

Chapter Two

Quote: Deuteronomy 13:4 (NIV)

1. Retrieved from http://adsabs.harvard.edu/full/1999JAHH....2...87H
2. Milliman, J., Czaplewski, A. J., & Ferguson, J. (2003). Workplace spirituality and employee work attitudes: An exploratory empirical assessment. Journal of organizational change management, 16(4), 426-447.

Chapter Three

Quote: Retrieved from www.brainyquote.com/quotes/inckl_b_hinckley_641100

1. Kellerman, B. (2008). Followership: How followers are creating change and changing leaders: Harvard Business School Press Boston.
2. 1 Corinthians 9:20
3. Ebstyne King, P. (2003). Religion and identity: The role of ideological, social, and spiritual contexts. Applied Developmental Science, 7(3), 197-204. (Page 198).
4. Martinez, R. J., Rogers, R., Yancey, G., & Singletary, J. (2011). Spiritual Capital in modern organizations. Journal of Biblical Integration in Business, 13(1).
5. Phipps, K. A. (2012). Spirituality and strategic leadership: The influence of spiritual beliefs on strategic decision making: JBE JBE. Journal of Business Ethics, 106(2), 177-189. doi:http://dx.doi.org.ezproxy.regent.edu:2048/10.1007/s10551-011-0988-5
6. Weick, K. E. (1979). Cognitive processes in organizations. Research in organizational behavior, 1(1), 41-74.
7. Case, P., & Gosling, J. (2010). The spiritual organization: Critical reflections on the instrumentality of workplace spirituality. Journal of Management, spirituality and Religion, 7(4), 257-282.
8. Den Hartog, D. N., House, R. J., Hanges, P. J., Ruiz-Quintanilla, S. A., Dorfman, P. W., Abdalla, I. A., ... & Akande, B. E. (1999). Culture specific and cross-culturally generalizable implicit leadership

theories: Are attributes of charismatic/transformational leadership universally endorsed? 1. The Leadership Quarterly, 10(2), 219-256

9. Massa, M. S. (1997). A Catholic for President: John F. Kennedy and the Secular Theology of the Houston Speech, 1960. *J. Church & St.*, 39, 297.

10. Ayandele, E. A. (1966). The missionary factor in northern Nigeria, 1870-1918. *Journal of the historical society of Nigeria*, 3(3), 503-522.

11. House, R. J., Hanges, P. J., Javidan, M., Dorfman, P. W., & Gupta, V. (Eds.). (2004). Culture, leadership, and organizations: The GLOBE study of 62 societies. Sage publications

12. Ibid

13. Kellerman, B. (2008). Followership: How followers are creating change and changing leaders: Harvard Business School Press Boston.

Chapter Four

Quote: Retrieved from the book Followership: The Manual by J. Michael Dumoulin

1. Kellerman, B. (2008). Followership: How followers are creating change and changing leaders: Harvard Business School Press Boston.

Chapter Five

Quote: Retrieved from https://www.goodreads.com/quotes/tag/relevant

1. John 1:35-42
2. Matthew 11:3
3. Matthew 11:5
4. Matthew 6:33

Chapter Six

Quote: Retrieved from https://www.goodreads.com/quotes/tag/relatability

1. Den Hartog, D. N., House, R. J., Hanges, P. J., Ruiz-Quintanilla, S. A., Dorfman, P. W., Abdalla, I. A., ... & Akande, B. E. (1999). Culture specific and cross-culturally generalizable implicit leadership

theories: Are attributes of charismatic/transformational leadership universally endorsed? 1. The Leadership Quarterly, 10(2), 219-256

Chapter Seven

Quote: Retrieved from https://libquotes.com/mencius/quote/lbn7p2o
1. Respect Written by Otis Redding (1965).
2. Romans 13:7
3. John 13:1-7
4. Excerpt retrieved from https://www.businessinsider.com/general-mattis-stories-2016-12?op=1

Chapter Eight

Quote retrieved from https://www.goodreads.com/quotes/search?commit=Search&page=25&q=Richie+Norton&utf8=%E2%9C%93
1. Svensson, G. (2005). Leadership performance in TQM: A contingency approach. The TQM Magazine, 17(6), 527-536. doi:http://dx.doi.org.ezproxy.regent.edu:2048/10.1108/09544780510627262

Chapter Nine

Quote retrieved from https://www.quotetab.com/quote/by-dieter-f-uchtdorf/ to-follow-christ-is-to-become-more-like-him-it-is-to-learn-from-his-character-a
1. Hillman, J. (1996). The soul's code: In search of character and calling. New York, NY: Random House (p.260)
2. Spears, L. C. (2010). Character and servant leadership: Ten characteristics of effective, caring leaders. The Journal of Virtues & Leadership, 1(1), 25-30.

Chapter Ten

Quote retrieved from https://www.brainyquote.com/quotes/peter_drucker_121122

1.   Meyer, J. P., & Allen, N. J. (1984). Testing the " side-bet theory" of organizational commitment: Some methodological considerations. Journal of applied psychology, 69(3), 372.

Chapter Eleven

Quote retrieved from https://www.brainyquote.com/quotes/curt_siodmak_398327

Chapter Twelve

Quote retrieved from https://genius.com/Simon-sinek-how-great-leaders-inspire-action-annotated

1.   Sinek, S. (2009). Start with why: How great leaders inspire everyone to take action. Penguin.
2.   Sims, R. R., & Brinkmann, J. (2003). Enron ethics (or: culture matters more than codes). Journal of Business ethics, 45(3), 243-256.
3.   Maccoby, M., Jody, H. G., & Ledeen, M. (2004). Leadership and the fear factor. MIT Sloan Management Review, 45(2), 14-18. Retrieved from http://eres.regent.edu:2048/login?url=https://search-proquest-com.ezproxy.regent.edu/docview/224963417?accountid=13479
4.   Aharonson-Daniel, L., Klein, Y., & Peleg, K. (2006). Suicide bombers form a new injury profile. Annals of surgery, 244(6), 1018.

Chapter Thirteen

Quote retrieved from Kellerman, B. (2008). How followers are creating change and changing leaders. Boston, MA: Harvard School Press.

1.   Psalm 139:14
2.   Matthew 10:39
3.   VanWhy, L. P. (2015). Development of the Authentic Followership Profile (AFP) test instrument (Doctoral dissertation, Regent University).

4. Kelley, R. E. (1992). The power of followership: How to create leaders people want to follow, and followers who lead themselves. Broadway Business.

Chapter Fourteen

1. Quote retrieved from https://www.wow4u.com/disappointment-quotes/

About The Author

Omokhai Imoukhuede (Ph.D, Regent University, MSc, Depaul) currently serves as the Resident Pastor at the CityLight International Assembly, Chicago south-side. In addition to his Pastoral calling, Pastor Omo's broad experience covers areas in Leadership, Followership, Group Dynamics, Technology, Entrepreneurship and Education.

Omokhai seeks to inspire, encourage and uplift individuals using various creative outlets like inspirational writings, trainings and speaking. He is also the author of the book *"Discovering Followership, Learn the Secrets of Walking Behind and Still Staying Ahead."*

Omokhai Imoukhuede is married to Osen who serves along with him at the CityLight International Church. They are blessed with four children Alina, Sophia, Hannah and Jeremiah-Stephen.

FOR MORE ON THIS AUTHOR

Website: www.omokhai.com

Books: www.omokhai.com/books

https://www.facebook.com/omokhai.imoukhuede/

https://www.instagram.com/omokhai/

@Omokhai1

For more information, email info@omokhai.com

Title: Following Well:

Understand The Followership Principles

That Make Life Work

ISBN 13: 978-0-578-73312-8

Copyright© 2020 by Omokhai Imoukhuede

Published by Limoux Designs Publishers

Chicago, IL 60620

Interior Design: Limoux Publishers

Made in the USA
Middletown, DE
21 August 2022